A COMPLETE INTRODUCTION TO

POODLES

All the information you need about selecting and keeping a Poodle—featuring sections on the breed's history, size varieties, training, health care, breeding, and showing.

Of all the purebred dog breeds, Poodles are among the most popular. Photo by Robert Pearcy.

──Anna Katherine Nicholas──

© 1987 by T.F.H. Publications, Inc.

Distributed in the UNITED STATES by T.F.H. Publications, Inc., 211 West Sylvania
Avenue, Neptune City, NJ 07753; in CANADA to the Pet Trade by H & L Pet Supplies Inc., 27 Kingston Crescent, Kitchener, Ontario N2B 2T6; Rolf C. Hagen Ltd.,
3225 Sartelon Street, Montreal 382 Quebec; in CANADA to the Book Trade by Mac-
millan of Canada (A Division of Canada Publishing Corporation), 164 Commander
Boulevard, Agincourt, Ontario M1S 3C7; in ENGLAND by T.F.H. Publications Lim-
ited, 4 Kier Park, Ascot, Berkshire SL5 7DS; in AUSTRALIA AND THE SOUTH PA-
CIFIC by T.F.H. (Australia) Pty. Ltd., Box 149, Brookvale 2100 N.S.W., Australia; in
NEW ZEALAND by Ross Haines & Son, Ltd., 18 Monmouth Street, Grey Lynn,
Auckland 2 New Zealand; in SINGAPORE AND MALAYSIA by MPH Distributors (S)
Pte., Ltd., 601 Sims Drive, #03/07/21, Singapore 1438; in the PHILIPPINES by Bio-
Research, 5 Lippay Street, San Lorenzo Village, Makati Rizal; in SOUTH AFRICA by
Multipet Pty. Ltd., 30 Turners Avenue, Durban 4001. Published by T.F.H. Publica-
tions Inc. Manufactured in the United States of America by T.F.H. Publications, Inc.

Contents

Poodle Character and Versatility

Life is never dull for a Poodle owner, which is probably one of the principal reasons why this breed has maintained its steady popularity year after year. Poodles remain among America's most widely owned breeds of dog and are, as well, highly regarded among dog fanciers around the world.

Poodles are merry companions who take great joy in life, with an enthusiasm they have been known to share with their people. I defy anyone to stay depressed watching a couple of Miniatures at play, with their amusing antics; or sharing the steadfast, dignified devotion of a Standard; or enjoying the big-dog characteristics of a Toy. Their delight in life is infectious, making them always interesting and companionable to have around.

Bright, intelligent, super-smart, and quick to learn—that is the Poodle. Small wonder that they have been used so frequently in areas where intelligence and aptitude are necessities of success. One finds them in circuses and vaudeville companies and on television shows where their "dancing," acrobatics, and other talents have been a delight to "children of all ages" for as long as these events have existed. They "dance" on their hind legs as though they had been born doing so, they train quickly, and they remember well. Their lightness of foot is also an advantage in their careers as entertainers, enabling them to perform with skill where less nimble dogs would never make it. Additionally, Poodles seem to truly like being on stage, which, considering their outgoing personalities and love of "hamming it up," I am sure they do.

You most likely will not be training your Poodle for a professional career as an entertainer; however, this instinct to perform makes training them an extremely easy task, should you be so inclined. The Poodle is one of the most responsive of all breeds to this type of training, the basic requirement on your part being a decent bit of patience. With a heritage of

This breed loves to play and to entertain. The learning of tricks comes quite easy, as you will soon learn. Photo by Sally Anne Thompson.

Poodles make perfect pets, since they are sweet and lovable, intelligent, and very devoted to their owners. Photo by Robert Pearcy.

dancing dogs and acrobatic dogs behind them, Poodles really seem to understand, instinctively, about performing. Shaking hands is a good starting point and is done simply by reaching for the right paw as you say clearly, "shake hands." "Catch" is learned by having the dog respond to throwing motions as you repeat the word. Then when the dog's full attention is on you, toss a toy or tidbit as you repeat the word. If the dog scrambles to pick up the object from the floor, grab it and repeat the exercise until he realizes it is from the air that you wish him to retrieve it. Poodles love to carry a newspaper or other small object in their mouths, so this is another easy trick to teach. It may be necessary to place the object between his jaws the first few times, but the Poodle will catch on fast if he is well praised and rewarded as he learns. The size of the object you give

Shaking hands comes naturally for Poodles. Photo by Sally Anne Thompson.

your dog should correspond to his size: never give a Standard Poodle a small item

that would be suitable for a Toy. The object should be large enough so that it cannot be swallowed. Probably the easiest "trick" of all for a Poodle is to "fetch" or "retrieve," these dogs having originally been water retrievers.

The sky is almost the limit if you start working this way with your Poodle, and if he has aptitude, you can teach him practically any trick or performance you may dream up.

No other breed offers the public so wide a choice of sizes, colors, and personalities as does the Poodle. Three sizes and half a dozen or so colors place the breed in the position of truly being able to provide an ideal dog for each owner. Add to this the many ways in which you can have your Poodle clipped, and I am certain readers will agree that this is, indeed, the breed which offers "something for everyone."

If you like a big dog who is sensible, reliable, steady, and the perfect companion-playmate-guardian for your children, the Standard Poodle is for you. Many people feel that the Standard is the most pleasant to live with of all the breeds, and the majority agree that this is the best all-around variety of Poodle. If you prefer a steady hunting companion who is an excellent retriever, remember that basically Poodles were developed as sporting and retrieving dogs and that the instinct is right there, as strongly as in many of the other retrieving breeds. Those fanciers who have tried developing this instinct have met with great success.

There are many who prefer the size of the smaller Poodles. Among medium-sized dogs, Miniature Poodles are smart, amusing, loving, and intelligent, with many endearing ways. They like having your companionship and your attention, and they ask for the latter whenever the opportunity arises. As for the Toys, these little dogs have the happy faculty of being small and lightweight, so if you travel a good deal, they can accompany you with a minimum of effort. I think of them as less "hyper" and lively than the Miniatures, but perhaps that description is typical of just the individuals I have known well. Toy Poodles are sweet pets, very intelligent, and absolutely ideal as personal companions to the owner whose lifestyle is geared to wanting a dog principally for that purpose. I do not recommend either Miniatures or Toys for young children, as their smallness makes them less able to endure, without being hurt, the sometimes unrealized extreme roughness of children's "play" with a canine pet. Obviously a dog so tiny as a Toy Poodle is bound to be fragile and therefore should be owned by and companion to grown-ups who

By teaching your Poodle tricks, you will provide him with an opportunity to exercise at the same time. Photo by Sally Anne Thompson.

will handle it with consideration. Some Miniatures are big enough and sturdy enough to get on well with children, but not all of them by any means.

The Standard Poodle makes a smashing country dog who will guard your home and share your interests and activities of suburban and country living. The Miniature is ideal in the suburbs or the city, while the Toy is unbeatable for anyone in the city, an apartment, or a condo. Toys are too small to generate nervousness in any but the most neurotic "anti-dog" person; and since those folks whose home responsibilities are few often are great travelers, here is a dog which travels well in a small carrier on a plane, is light enough to pick up and carry easily, yet combines all the best features of the wonderful breed he represents in its smallest form.

Their extreme curiosity and alertness give Poodles an almost uncanny sense of hearing. They know when someone is approaching, even before anyone else in

Your local pet shop stocks all sorts of dog beds in a variety of shapes, sizes, colors, and materials. Photo by Barbara Lockwood.

the household is aware, sounding the news with their sharp, quick bark. We find with our own Miniatures that they announce approaching cars and people from nearly the length of a city block away, and when they make

these announcements, they are invariably right. Thus they make splendid watch dogs, all three varieties of them, in the area of greatest importance in watch-dogging—that of spreading the word. It is not so important that a dog be equipped and prepared to chew up an intruder, something most of us wish in only the most extreme and dangerous circumstances. We simply want a possible intruder to change his mind and go away. The thing most likely to bring about this result is noise, such as that provided by a reliable dog's persistent barking. Always investigate the barking, as this will call attention to the prowler's presence and perhaps result in his discovery, or, still better, his departure. Any of the Poodle varieties can and do provide this service well.

The hunting spirit is far stronger in Poodles than is generally realized. These elegant looking, unconcernedly groomed dogs are quick on the trigger when it comes to dispatching a rat, doing so with all the dexterity one looks for in a terrier. This realization came to us with somewhat of a shock the evening when our

Facing page: *Leslie Nelinson owns this handsome pair of Standard Poodles shown in the Sporting clip style. The face, throat, feet, and base of the tail are shaved, while the rest of their coat is left long. Photo by Isabelle Francais.*

apricot Miniature puppy proudly carried in and presented to us an obviously lust-killed rat. Upon inquiry to numerous of our Poodle-owning friends, we were advised that this is by no means an isolated occurrence as Poodles are "great hunters"!

The fastidiousness of Poodles makes them trustworthy and ideal house dogs, to the point that they can usually be taken quite safely to other people's

One couldn't want a better watchdog for the children than a Poodle. Photo by Sally Anne Thompson.

homes, or wherever else we ourselves may go that dogs are welcome. They seem aware of their elegance and on social occasions clearly make their behavior fit their appearance. They love visiting, too, being great "people fanciers."

Among the many assets of a Poodle is the tremendously important one to many people that this is a breed which does not shed and can, almost without exception, share the home of a person who is allergic to dog hair and is thus unable to own most breeds. I have known this to be true on literally hundreds of occasions—people who think they must be deprived of dog ownership, discovering that they can, indeed, share life with a Poodle and feel no ill results. This is surely a tremendous boon to dog lovers who hate being without a dog! Although some folks may be immediately allergic to the majority of dogs, I have never known such a person who has tried a Poodle without success, nor of one who has suffered allergy problems due to a Poodle's presence in the home. Even if allergy is no problem for you, it is great not to have dog hair all over your rugs, furniture, and clothes. This is just one more reason why Poodles are so popular with the pet-owning public.

Something else nice about Poodles who are to share your home as family companions is their longevity. Properly cared for and barring accidents, your Poodle should live to his mid-teens; occasionally some dogs live longer. Considering the shortness of the canine lifetime, and the early age which is considered "old" in numerous breeds, this is a decided asset if you are taking on a dog for companionship to whom you will undoubtedly become closely attached as the years you spend together pass. What an added heartache if the dog is only to be with you eight or nine years, as is the case in some breeds, most particularly the very large breeds. At least the sadness of losing a pet is eased slightly if one can feel that this animal enjoyed a long, happy canine lifetime, which many Poodles have done.

Under the heading of "things you can do with your Poodle" comes, right at the top of the list, working with him in obedience training. Every dog of every breed for his own safety should be taught the basic obedience exercises. "Sit," "stay," "heel," "down," and "come" are all directives which sometime may save your dog's life if the commands are given and obeyed promptly; thus it is imperative that obedience training be started at an early age. You will be able to locate training classes and obedience match shows in your area, wherever you may live. Take advantage of this by "joining up" and working with your dog as he approaches age six months, although by this time the two of you should have the basics pretty well mastered by working at home for ten- or fifteen-minute intervals a day. If you and the puppy do well and enjoy the training classes

"Mom, may I have all three of them?" this youngster (top) seems to be saying. Note the difference in size between the white Standard Poodle on his hindlegs and the black Miniature Poodle leaping in the air (bottom). Photos by Sally Anne Thompson.

and obedience matches, you are ready to try your hand at real obedience competition. So talented are Poodles in obedience work that you will notice a large number of them with impressive obedience degrees on their record, indicated by such letters as C.D., C.D.X., U.D., T.D., etc., following their names. These signify degrees earned in formal obedience competition, as do the letters OTCh. preceding the name of the dog. You can obtain information on the obedience trials in your area through the person from whom your Poodle was purchased or through the American Kennel Club, 51 Madison Avenue, New York, New York 10010. Perhaps your veterinarian can recommend someone who is an obedience trial participant.

Poodles are agreeable with other household pets if properly introduced. Of course if both are youngsters, it is that much easier, although an older dog will almost without exception accept a new canine friend or a feline one if the introduction is handled carefully. One should not make the older pet feel pushed into the background by the youngster's arrival; rather he should be lavished with even more than his usual share of affection until the strangeness of a new household member has worn off. Then both animals should be equal recipients of love and petting.

There are breeders who feel

If introduced properly at an early age, there is no reason why your Poodle cannot become friends with other pets in your household.

that the Poodle colors are accompanied by separate personalities. By this criterion, the apricots, browns, and silvers are known for being more "skittery" than the blacks and the whites. I have owned both apricot and

chocolate Miniatures and can see nothing strange about the personality of either color. Perhaps it is more a matter of their home environment or the ownership to which these dogs are accustomed. The beauty of the blacks and whites is undeniable, but to many people, the apricots are without peer. Then, of course, there are the "silver Miniature" fans to whom these dogs are the epitome of Poodle perfection. Whatever

The height of a Toy Poodle, such as this white one, should be ten inches or less from the highest point of the shoulders.

their color, Poodles retain the quality of temperament for which they have been bred through the years and many generations. So choose whatever color Poodle you like best; you will find your dog will be everything one expects in this breed.

Origin and Early History

Contrary to the belief of many people, Poodles are not a French breed of dog, although so popular did they become there that they were eventually known as "the national dog of France." Actually the breed is one of those to have originated in Germany, where it was named "Pudel," owing to its love of "splashing in water" which is known there as "pudelin."

Thus we become aware that Poodles are water dogs who made their way into France in the company of German troops and who soon established themselves as admirable, useful, intelligent dogs with a great tendency to swim whenever possible and to retrieve well on land or in water. The strength of these dogs, a good nose, and superb intelligence brought them into many uses, a major one of which was duck hunting. So closely did the breed become associated with duck hunters and the retrieving of these birds that they were called, in France, "Chien canne" or "Caniche," both derivatives of the French name for *duck*, "canard."

In order to enable the dogs to swim and retrieve more freely, a "lion clip" was created for these dogs. The heavy coat was clipped away over the hindquarters and

Miniature Poodle owned by Marjorie McCarthy. Photo by Isabelle Francais.

hips, reducing the burden of wet hair. This lion clip has remained with the dogs over many generations, adding not only to their working freedom, but also to the balance and elegance of appearance thus created in our modern Poodles.

In the beginning, all Poodles were Standards. The Miniatures were created by breeding down from the smaller of these, the Toys by breeding the smaller Miniatures with a breed known as "Toy Poodles." The latter did not, however, excel in true Poodle type as we have come to know it today.

Russia, another country where the earlier Poodles were popular, drew up its own breed standard (written description of these dogs) back in the early days. Germany and France each had their own standards too, and only three colors were acceptable in these three countries, with Germany preferring the browns, France the whites, and Russia the blacks. Eventually France developed the blues and the silvers. Now many breathtaking colors, apricot being among the most popular, have been created by astute breeders.

As one of the early canine breeds, Poodles have been used in the foundation and in the improvement of other former breeds as well. For example, a "Poodle cross" was created in Germany for no understandable reason to

the fanciers who followed; and we have read references to "Poodle Pointers," "Poodle Griffons," and "Poodle Pomeranians," which also seem to have led nowhere. There is no denying the Poodle influence, however, as noted in the conformation coat and type of the Curly-Coated Retriever and the Irish Water Spaniel, breeds which both bear a strong resemblance to Poodles.

Poodle talents are diversified, and the dogs are known and loved for several in addition to their usefulness in retrieving. The latter is, after all, primarily work for the larger (Standard) size dogs. But there is another Poodle of distinguished accomplishment, too, a little dog known as the "Truffle Poodle" who was small of size and light of foot. He made himself extremely useful in France, England, Germany, and Spain by locating and digging up the edible fungus known as the truffle, regarded in these countries as a rare, expensive, and coveted delicacy. Quick sure-footedness, a keen sense of smell, and a light touch with the paw so as not to damage or break the delicate fungus were the requisites for a successful Truffle Poodle.

Facing page: *As far as color is concerned, Poodles have something to offer everyone. Apricot and brown, for example, have become quite popular. Photo by Robert Pearcy.*

These little dogs were considered to be primarily Poodles, although some fanciers felt that there was a slight terrier outcross, an opinion debated on more than one occasion. Quite possibly this Truffle Poodle is an early ancestor of the original Toy Poodle, which was a separate breed until well into the first half of the twentieth century when it was combined with small Miniature Poodles to create the smallest of the three Poodle varieties.

Truffle Poodles were highly esteemed in Great Britain where they and their services were greatly in demand at World War I. These little dogs in appearance were parti-colored Poodles (a disqualification by present-day standards), usually white with a black head and tail plus sometimes a few black spots on the body. These parti-colored dogs were shown in England under their own classification, and widely admired, at the Botanical Gardens and other prestigious dog shows. A gentleman named Mr. Cowan was an especially successful competitor with several of his, while another lovely dog named Peter, whose owner was not identified, was written

In fair weather, many dog shows are held out of doors. This particular show is taking place in England. Photo by Sally Anne Thompson.

high prices, especially from the time of the late nineteenth century until the beginning of

up as having a beautifully long, lean head of correct type and the typical short back. Eventually brown-and-white dogs as well as lemon-and-white were also seen among the white-with-black Truffle Poodles. Special note has been made of their huge coats and the latter's hard coat texture.

From the first century onward to the present day, Poodles have been popular with great and talented artists. Consequently the collecting of Poodle drawings, paintings, sculptures (bronzes, porcelains, etc.), and other Poodle memorabilia is a fascinating and rewarding hobby in which many Poodle enthusiasts are pleasurably involved.

Even in those long ago days, when dogs were thought of primarily in connection with their working qualities, Poodles were endearing themselves to ladies of fashion as especially loving and interesting pets. Also, they were known both privately and publicly as entertainers who provided great amusement for their audience, whether it be at the circus or by command at home. Poodle troupes are among the world's most respected canine entertainers, having real talent for acrobatics, plus a keen intelligence.

Teach your child how to respect and care for his or her dog, not handle it as though it were a plaything. Photo by Tom Caravaglia.

DEVELOPMENT OF THE POODLE

Poodles were warmly welcomed to England during the latter part of the nineteenth century, with the first Specialty club for the breed established there in 1886. Some 40 years later the Curly Poodle Club, the Miniature Poodle Club, and the International Poodle Club came into being, the latter holding its first Specialty show in 1933 with 82 Poodles for a total of 202 entries. This was the largest Poodle Specialty until that time.

In England and elsewhere Poodle popularity steadily increased throughout the early 1900s. In the beginning the corded type of Poodle coat was the most admired in the show ring, a situation which changed, however, as more and more pet owners grew to prefer the curly coats which are easier to care for. Curly-coated Poodles are still the more popular of the two today, with the appearance of an occasional corded variety which excites interest and curiosity among people who have never previously seen one. The early corded dogs were, indeed, handsome; but the growing of the cords and keeping them neat and clean was a project to which many people could not possibly dedicate the time and effort involved.

The denial of the English Poodle breeders' petition for a separation of cordeds and curlys, each having its own stud book, led to the formation of the Curly Poodle Club to help promote increasing interest in coats of that type. The eventual result was that cordeds gradually disappeared from the show ring.

The French standard had always been the preferred standard among English Poodle breeders. However, some minor differences of opinion which arose just prior to the 1930s caused Britain's Curly Poodle Club to abandon that standard and create a new one of its own. It is from the latter that the Poodle Club of America standard was derived, this occurring in the 1930s shortly after the club's formation.

Poodles were raised and exhibited in the United States just prior to World War I, with show classification in those days divided by coat type rather than by size. Miniature and Standard Poodles competed together as one breed, while Toys were classified as an entirely different breed. Both Poodles and Toy Poodles had numerous devoted fans during the early 1900s. There was but a single Poodle registration in 1890, two in 1891, and 20 in 1893. By 1915, 245 Poodles were registered with no Toy registrations. At the end of World War I, in 1918, the number plummeted to 47 Poodles, along with two Toy registrations.

The following decades were a series of triumphs for Poodles around the world: the recognition of Miniatures as a separate variety of startling success; the creation of Toy Poodles as yet another variety; and the steady quality and position of the Standards all helped to place the breed at the top in dog-show circles and in number of registrations. Many dedicated people worked intelligently and hard to create the modern-day Poodle. For those of you who want more of an "in depth" coverage on Poodles, I suggest you purchase another of my books, *The Book of the Poodle*, published, as is this one, by T.F.H. Publications, Inc. This large-format volume includes hundreds of pages of Poodle world history, photos, and invaluable information for any Poodle owner anxious to really know all about the breed.

Throughout Europe, in Canada, in Japan, in Australia,

Your Poodle will need regular grooming attention to keep his coat in good condition, free of tangles and mats. You must periodically brush, clip, and bathe him or have a professional groomer do this for you. Photo by Fritz Prenzel.

and in South America outstanding Poodles are being raised and shown. Poodles of true quality and great beauty are to be found in all of these places, based, in many cases, on the finest imported stock and sensible, well-thought-out breeding programs.

Physical Characteristics of the Breed

One's first impression upon looking at a Poodle is that of elegance and poise, combined with activity . . . a distinctive dog of a dignity peculiar to himself alone. Sound moving and carrying himself with gaiety and pride, the Poodle impresses one with good balance and alertness, well-proportioned squareness of build, and intelligence of expression.

Whether the variety one regards is a Standard, measuring 15 inches or more at the highest point of withers; a Miniature, more than 10 but less than 15 inches tall at highest point of withers; or a Toy, 10 inches or less at the withers; the

Two-year-old Miniature. One of the nice features of the Poodle coat is that it does not shed, making this breed perfect for people who are allergic to dog hair. Photo by Tom Caravaglia.

requisites are the same. Feature by feature, these three varieties are the same dog in three different size packages.

The Poodle head is moderately rounded in skull with a definite but slight stop. Cheekbones are flat, the skull measuring almost an equal distance from stop to occiput as the muzzle from stop to tip of nose. The muzzle is long, lean, and fine, slightly chiseled beneath the eyes. It should be strong with no "lippiness," the chin sufficiently definite to preclude snipiness. Strong, white teeth must meet in a "scissors" bite, whereby the inner tips of the upper incisors touch the outer tips of the lower incisors.

Poodle eyes should be oval in shape, very dark, and set wide enough apart to create an intelligent expression. Ears, set just below eye level, hang close to the head. The ear leather is thickly feathered, long and wide.

A well-proportioned neck, long and sufficiently strong to carry the head with height and dignity, rises from strong, smoothly-muscled shoulders. Skin on the throat should be snug with no dewlap. The shoulder blade should be well laid back and of approximately the same length as the upper foreleg.

The length of the Poodle's body should measure, from breastbone to point of rump, approximately the height from highest point of withers to the ground. The chest is deep and moderately wide with the ribs well sprung. The topline is level, neither roached nor sloping, from the highest

Champion Bel Tor Carefree, a lovely brown Standard, bred and owned by Mrs. J. A. Mason. In browns, the eyes, eyerims, lips, nose, and toenails should also be brown.

point of the shoulder blade to the base of the tail. There should, however, be a slight hollow immediately behind the shoulder. The loin is short, broad, and muscular.

The tail should be straight, set on high and carried up, and docked at sufficient length to assure a balanced outline.

Forelegs are straight and parallel when viewed from the front, elbow directly below the highest point of the shoulder

27

when viewed from the side. Bone and muscle of both forelegs and hindlegs should be in proportion to the size of the dog. Pasterns on forelegs should be strong. Viewed from behind, the rear legs are straight and parallel. They should be muscular with width in the region of the well-bent stifles. The femur and tibia are about equal in length, hock to heel short and perpendicular to the ground. When standing, the rear toes are only slightly behind the point of rump, with hindquarter angulation balancing to that of the forequarters.

Poodle feet, correctly, are small and oval in shape. The toes are well arched and nicely cushioned by thick, firm pads. Nails should be short but not excessively shortened. Feet should turn neither in nor out. Dewclaws may be removed.

If your Poodle is to be shown, it must be in one of the required clips as described in the breed standard. The Poodle coat should be of a naturally harsh texture, dense throughout, and curly. There is also a corded coat known in Poodles (popular in historic times), in which the hair hangs in tight, even cords of varying lengths that are longer on the mane, body, head, and ears but shorter on the puffs, bracelets, and pompoms.

The Poodle coat must be of an even, solid color at the skin. In blues, grays, silvers, browns, cafe-au-laits, apricots, and creams, the coat may show varying shades of the same color, especially in the form of darker featherings of the ears and in the tipping of the ruff. Although clear colors are preferable, such natural variations in the shading of the coat are not to be considered a fault.

Brown and cafe-au-lait Poodles have liver-colored noses, eye rims, and lips, dark toenails, and dark amber eyes. Black, blue, gray, silver, cream, and white Poodles have black noses, eye rims, and lips, black or self-colored toenails, and very dark eyes. In the apricots the foregoing coloring is preferred; liver-colored noses, eye rims, and lips, along with amber eyes, are permitted but not preferred.

In motion, the Poodle travels in a straightforward trot with light, springy action and strong hindquarter drive. Sound and effortless in movement, the dog's head and tail are carried high, creating a picture of elegant style.

A Poodle will be disqualified from competition in the show ring if appearing in *any* style clip other than the Puppy clip (for puppies only), the English Saddle clip, the Continental clip, or, in special situations, the Sporting clip. Parti-color Poodles shall be disqualified, as shall Poodles who are not within the size range of their Variety.

Grooming Your Poodle

From the time that your Poodle is a tiny puppy until he reaches old age, coat care and grooming will be a necessary part of his life. Thus the earlier the puppy becomes accustomed to the processes this involves, the better for all concerned as the puppy matures. The grooming of a Poodle ranges from simple to complicated, depending on whether we are talking of a pet or of a show dog. In the latter case, time spent on the grooming table can seem mighty tedious to a dog whose "basic training" has not included preparation for it.

As soon as a puppy is a couple of weeks old, it should become accustomed to the sound and feel of electric clippers; without this equipment, a Poodle cannot be "done" properly. Even the simplest of styles involves some clipping on the dog, the show clips and the fancy pet styles requiring a considerable amount. Astute Poodle breeders take precationary measures to reduce the fear or trauma associated with the sound of electric clippers by conditioning their puppies to the noise when they are just a few days old. The basic steps consist of making the roar of the clippers a normal sound, running them frequently in the puppies' room, and gradually moving nearer until finally the clippers are held gently against each pup's face. This way a puppy gets the "feel" of

Many Poodle owners have their dogs done by professional groomers. You may want to discuss styles and clips with the groomer before he or she works on your dog. Loose hairs and ragged edges are smoothed down with scissors (top). The top of the head is rounded (bottom), again using scissors. Keep in mind that if you plan to show your Poodle, he must be presented in only those clips rocognized in the Poodle breed standard of perfection, namely, the Continental clip, the English Saddle clip, the Puppy clip, and the Sporting clip. A Poodle shown in any other clip will be disqualifed. Photos by Sally Anne Thompson.

the clippers and in so doing learns that they present no harm. Then the clippers are used to gently clear away hair on the muzzle. Always be light in your touch and careful not to risk cutting or "burning" the puppy's skin by pressing too hard.

Young puppies should grow accustomed to being brushed gently with a small "pin brush" and to having a course-toothed metal comb run through their coat, both gently and with care, at an early age. Brushing *always* should be done in even rows from the skin to the tips of the hair, and you should ascertain that no sections are skipped nor that any premature tangles are overlooked. A wide-toothed comb should be used on the dog to help separate any mats which may be forming.

Poodle ears, like those of all heavily-coated breeds, need special attention. Hairs within the ear grow and must be plucked out periodically with a pair of tweezers. Done quickly, gently, and firmly, the plucking will not hurt your dog. Never overlook this routine procedure; otherwise accumulated earwax will settle in the roots of these hairs, making a cozy nest for ear mites and causing other complications. A puppy may object at first, but soon he will become accustomed to this important grooming ritual. Excessive scratching of an ear, head shaking, or holding the head to one side usually indicates an ear problem which should be checked by your veterinarian at once.

Toenails are another area where grooming should start at an early age, as a nursing puppy can hurt or actually damage his mother's teats if he holds on with pin-like nail tips. During the nursing period, only the tips of the nails should be clipped to dull their sharpness. An older Poodle, as well, will need periodic attention to the nails.

Many dog groomers often brush the hair on top of the head into a long topknot and twist a rubber band around it to hold it back away from the dog's face.

BATHING

If your Poodle puppy needs a bath, give it to him. Do so in a basin of comfortably warm water, soaking the coat with a rubber spray hose and using a shampoo made especially for dogs. Pat and squeeze the shampoo into the coat; DO NOT RUB, as rubbing wet Poodle hair causes tangles. Rinse by running clear water over the pup until all traces of soap are gone, then BLOT dry with a soft towel. Finish with a hair dryer. Incidentally, before bathing your Poodle, whether he is a puppy or an adult, first put a drop of castor oil in each eye (to prevent irritation of soap in the eyes) and a wad of cotton in each ear (to prevent water from entering the ear canals) prior to soaping the dog.

Many people like to use a cream rinse on their Poodles after the shampoo as a finishing touch. This should be carefully selected (there are many on the market), and if you are not pleased with the first one, try others until you find the one most suitable for your dog's coat. Use these products, as directed, after the coat has been thoroughly rinsed of soap.

Remember, now, the importance of never rubbing wet Poodle fur. To wash and rinse the coat, squeeze it between the palms and fingers; then blot and blow dry. In drying with an electric hair blower, the best way is to place the puppy or dog on the grooming table, making sure that the air coming from the blower is a comfortable warmth and that it does not work too hot as it runs, and to brush the coat at the same time. Right then, the puppy's

Some people love Poodles so much that they keep several as household companions. These famous obedience winners belong to Mrs. Joseph Longo of Rye Kennels.

education in lying on a table begins, as you teach him to stay first on one side, then the other side, and then to stand or sit quietly as you complete the job. A grooming post with a loop that fastens around the dog's neck so that he stays still is particularly useful. Check your local pet shop for a portable post that attaches to a table.

As your Poodle grows from puppyhood, something larger than a basin will be needed to accommodate the bath procedure: a large, deep sink will be suitable for full-grown Toys and Miniatures, while a full-sized bathtub will suffice for Standards.

A word about the above referenced grooming table: this is a rubber-topped table which comes in sizes appropriate for your variety of Poodle. The ribbed-rubber surface prevents slipping, giving the dog a feeling of security. The table should be equipped with a post, to which can be attached a loop (or "noose") for slipping around the dog's neck. This keeps him securely in place, making your work easier. Everyone owning a breed of dog that needs constant coat care should also own a grooming table, which, when not in use, can be folded up and stored away. Such a collapsible model can also be taken along to dog shows. Even for puppies, this type of table is the safest place on which to perform grooming duties; the dogs grow accustomed to being on the table and they relax comfortably while you work.

Brushing your dog while blow-drying him is the ideal way to groom and dry your Poodle at the same time. Aim the dryer at the part of the dog on which you are working, and then brush as he blows dry. *As you do this, always be alert for signs of tangling hair or the beginning of mats.* This means that you should carefully check and examine the underarms, between the hindlegs, and behind the ears, these being especially vulnerable "trouble spots." For this brushing, you should be using a good-quality pin brush and carefully brushing the entire length of hair from skin to tip. Make methodical lines as you go along.

The Dog Show World

Quality in the sense of "show quality" is determined by various factors such as the dog's health, physical condition, temperament, ability to move, and appearance. Breeders trying to breed show dogs are attempting to produce animals which come as close as possible to the word description of perfection as set out in the breed standard.

Keep in mind that dog show terminology varies from one place to another and even from one time to another. If you plan to show your dog, it always makes sense to check with your local or national breed club or with the national dog registry for the most complete, most up-to-date information regarding dog show regulations. In Great Britain, for example, match shows are known as limit shows. Age limit also differs, as dogs less than six months old may not be shown in Britain. Additionally, Britain has no point system for dogs, rather the dogs compete for championship certificates (C.C.s). Thus, point shows are known as championship shows in Great Britain.

MATCH SHOWS

One of the best ways to see

If you plan to show your Poodle, keep in mind the dog's age. In the United States, dogs less than two months cannot be shown. Dogs shown in Great Britain must be no less than six months.

if your puppy has championship potential is to attend a match show which is usually organized by the local kennel club or breed specialty club. Such shows provide a useful learning experience for the amateur and they offer you the opportunity to see how well your dog measures up to others being shown. There you can mingle with owners and professional handlers and pick up basic guidelines in showmanship, performance, and procedure. You can learn a great deal merely by closely observing the professional handlers performing in the ring.

The age limit is usually reduced to two months at match shows so that puppies can have four months of training before they compete in the regular shows when they reach six months. This time also helps them to overcome any "crowd nervousness." As class categories are the same as those included at a regular show, much experience can be gained in this informal atmosphere. Entry fees are low and paid at the door.

You may want to invest in a grooming table if you plan to show your dog. The post adjusts to the height of your dog, while the loop fastens to his neck to keep him still.

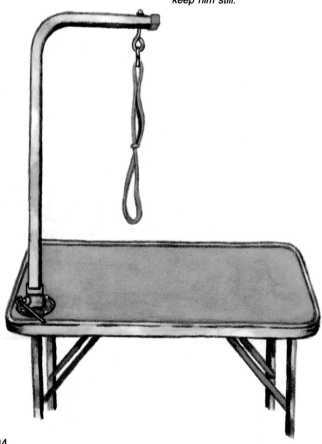

Before you go to a show, your dog should be trained to gait at a trot beside you, with head up and in a straight line. In the ring you will have to gait around the edge with other dogs and then individually up and down the center runner. In addition, the dog must stand for examination by the judge, who will look at him closely and feel his head and body structure. He should be taught to stand squarely, hind feet slightly back and head up. He must hold the pose when you place his feet, and he must show a lively interest when you "bait" him, *i.e.,* tempt him with a piece of boiled liver or a small squeak toy.

There are all sorts of grooming products, available at most pet shops, that will help keep your dog's coat in top condition.

Check your dog's nails periodically; if they need to be trimmed, use a pet nail clipper.

COAT
CONDITIONER
FOR DOGS

If your puppy receives praise and words of encouragement from the judges and other knowledgeable people, then you can begin to dream of Westminster or Crufts. It is always useful to visit such prestigious shows to see the best examples of all the various breeds.

After you have taken some handling lessons yourself, or employed a professional handler, the next step is participation in the point shows where you can earn points toward your dog's championship.

POINT SHOWS

Unlike match shows where your dog was judged on ring behavior, at point shows he will be judged on conformation to his breed standard. It is advisable to write to your national dog

The easiest way to bathe your Poodle, no matter what his size, is to place him in a large tub.

registry for information on how to register your dog and apply to dog shows. Below are the names and addresses of registries in the United States, Canada, Great Britain, and Australia.

The American Kennel Club
51 Madison Avenue
New York, NY 10010

The Canadian Kennel Club
111 Eglinton Avenue East
Toronto, Ontario M6S 4V7
Canada

The Kennel Club of Great Britain
1 Clarges Street
Piccadilly, London, W1Y 8AB, England

The Australian Kennel Club
Royal Show Grounds
Ascot Vale, Victoria, Australia

Your local kennel club can provide you with the names and addresses of the show-giving superintendents (or show secretaries) near you, who will be staging the club's dog show for them, and where you must write for an official entry form. The forms will be mailed in a pamphlet called the "premium list" which will include the names of the judges for each breed, a list of the prizes and trophies, the names and addresses of the show-giving club, where the show will be held, as well as the rules and required procedure. Make certain that you fill in the form clearly and carefully and mail it in plenty of time.

Before then, however, you will have to decide in which classes your dog should compete. In the United States these are: Puppy, Novice, Bred-by-Exhibitor, American-bred and Open.

Puppy Classes are for dogs six months of age and over but under twelve months which are not champions. The age of a dog shall be calculated up to and inclusive of the first day of the show.

The *Novice Class* is for dogs six months of age and over, whelped in the United States or Canada, which have not, prior to the official closing date for entries, won three first prizes in the Novice Class, a first prize in Bred-by-Exhibitor, American-bred or

Poodles get along well with other animals, provided both parties are properly introduced (top). The mother of this adorable puppy (bottom) looks on as her youngster is being weaned.

Open Class or one or more points toward championship. In Britain, of course, dogs competing in the Novice Class must have been whelped in Britain.

The *Bred-by-Exhibitor Class* is for dogs whelped in the U.S.A. or, if individually registered in the American Kennel Club Stud Book, for dogs in Canada that are six months of age and over. They must not be champions (although they may be in Britain), and must be owned wholly or in part by the person or the spouse of the person who was the breeder or one of the breeders of record. Dogs in this class must be handled by an owner or by a member of the immediate family of the owner. (This is not the case, however, in Britain.) Members of an immediate family for this purpose are: husband, wife, father, mother, son, daughter, brother and sister. This class has been referred to as the "breeder's showcase" as it is the one where the breeders can be justly proud of their achievements.

The *American-bred Class* is for all dogs (except champions) six months of age or over, whelped in the U.S.A. by reason of a mating that took place in the U.S.A.

The *Open Class* is for any dog six months of age or over, except in a member specialty club show held only for American-bred dogs, in which case the class is for American-bred dogs only.

In the United States and Canada, one does not enter the *Winners Class.* One earns the right to compete in it by

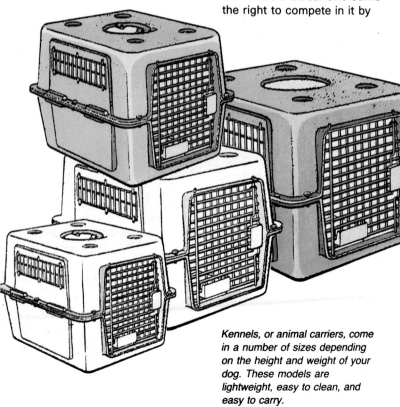

Kennels, or animal carriers, come in a number of sizes depending on the height and weight of your dog. These models are lightweight, easy to clean, and easy to carry.

winning first prize in one of the above classes. Winners Dog and Winners Bitch are the awards which carry points toward championship with them. Also designated by the judge are the Reserve Winners Dog and the Reserve Winners Bitch (in Britain these are designated Reserve C.C. Dog and Reserve C.C. Bitch) but they do not receive any points. This award means simply that the dog or bitch receiving it are standing "in reserve" should the Winners Dog or Winners Bitch be disallowed through any technicality in the official show rules and regulations.

Electric nail groomers help smooth your dog's rough nail edges.

The dog and bitch then compete against each other for Best of Winners, and they also vie with the champions in the Specials Class for Best of Breed and for Best of Opposite Sex to Best of Breed. In Britain, the Reserve C.C. winners compete against each other for Best of Breed, not Best of Winners.

Best of Breed is the highest-placing dog in a given breed, and that winner then represents the particular breed in Group competition. Groups include: Sporting Dogs, Herding Dogs, Hounds, Working Dogs, Terriers, Toys, and Non-sporting Dogs. The judge of each Group selects first, second, third, and fourth place among the Best of Breed winners within specific Groups. First-place winners in each Group then compete for

Best in Show.

A scale of points is printed in each dog-show catalog, and the number of points awarded in a breed depends on the number of dogs shown in competition. A win of three or more points at a show is called a "major." To attain championship, a dog must win a total of fifteen points under at least three different

Simply press each nail against the nail groomer and let the revolving dressing stone do the work.

judges, and included in those fifteen points must be two majors (each under a different judge). A dog that accumulates fifteen points and no majors does not qualify for championship. A dog must win in keen competition. (This is the case in the United States but not in Great Britain. As there is no point system in Britain, it doesn't matter how many dogs are shown in competition. Championship Certificates are awarded at the discretion of the Judge, however few dogs are competing.)

PRE-SHOW PREPARATIONS

As a very basic guide, the following list has been compiled to help you with your preparations for your first point show: the identification ticket sent by the show superintendent, a grooming table, a sturdy tack box in which to carry your dog's grooming tools, a leash to fasten him to the bench or stall and another show lead, your first aid kit, packaged "dog treats," and a supply of food and water for man and beast. Take the largest thermos you can find and a water dish. Remember to feed your dog after the show, not before, and make certain that he exercises and relieves himself before he enters the ring. Many experts think that an exercise pen is mandatory to eliminate the risk of exposing your dog to any diseases in the common exercise ground at shows, but before you bring one along, check the show rules to see if these are allowed. Moreover, exercise pens are useful as places where your dog can

Show training should begin when a Poodle is just a puppy so that he becomes accustomed to the various procedures.

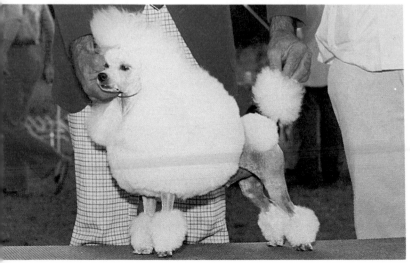

stretch out or rest during your travels or at a motel.

Even take time to think about what you are going to wear on the big day; sports clothes and low-heeled, comfortable shoes are the best. You certainly do not want to wear anything that would distract the judge's attention from your dog; you should merely provide an attractive background for him.

Although your knees may be trembling, try to appear self-confident as you gait (move) and set up the dog. The judging routine usually begins when the judge asks that the dogs be gaited in a circle around the ring while he observes their style, topline, head and tail carriage, reach and drive, and general balance. Avoid going too close to the dog in front of you. Make certain that the judge has an unrestricted view of your dog by keeping him on the inside of the circle, between you and the judge.

Pet Poodles should be groomed regularly; however, show-quality Poodles, such as the ones you see here, need extra special attention to keep them in top condition. Photo by Sally Anne Thompson.

DOG SHOW ETIQUETTE

There are a few "golden rules" to be followed at dog shows which are worth mentioning at this stage. First of all, you are responsible for the behavior of your dog at all times. Keep your dog with you until the showing and keep him under control at all times. Constant vigilance is necessary as thefts have been known at dog shows, as well as poisoning and physical abuse of the animals by jealous exhibitors. You do not want your dog to become involved in a dog fight or taken for a walk by an irresponsible child or one too young to discipline him. In other words, you must not let your dog out of your sight.

Another golden rule is to be punctual; do not be late for your class. Remember that in the ring you must not communicate with the judge or fellow competitors. Watch the judge carefully and follow his instructions. Bear in mind that the ring is not the place to discipline or train your dog; it is too late at this stage! Whatever the judge's decision, accept it with good grace whether you win or lose.

The New Family Member

At long last, the day you have all been waiting for, your new puppy will make its grand entrance into your home. Before you bring your companion to its new residence, however, you must plan carefully for its arrival. Keep in mind that the puppy will need time to adjust to life with a different owner. He may seem a bit apprehensive about the strange surroundings in which he finds himself, having spent the first few weeks of life with his dam and littermates, but in a couple of days, with love and patience on your part, the transition will be complete.

First impressions are important, especially from the puppy's point of view, and these may very well set the pattern of his future relationship with you. You must be consistent, always, in the way you handle your pet so that he learns what is expected of him. He must come to trust and respect you as his keeper and master. Provide him with proper care and attention, and you will be rewarded with a loyal companion for many years. Considering the needs of your puppy and planning ahead will surely make the change from his former home to his new one easier.

ADVANCE PREPARATION

In preparing for your puppy's arrival, perhaps more important than anything else is to find out from the seller how the pup was maintained. What brand of food was offered and when and how often was the puppy fed? Has the pup been housebroken; if so, what method was employed? Attempt to continue whatever routine was started by the person from whom you bought your

Many airlines supply animal carriers for you to purchase; these are necessary if you plan to ship your dog by air.

puppy, then, gradually, you can make those changes that suit you and your lifestyle. If, for example, the puppy has been paper trained, plan to stock up on newspaper. Place this newspaper toilet facility in a selected spot so that your puppy learns to use the designated area as its "bathroom." And keep on hand a supply of the dog food to which he is accustomed, as

check-ups, inoculations, and prompt medical attention in case of illness or an emergency. Find out if the animal you have selected has been vaccinated against

a sudden switch to new food could cause digestive upsets.

Another consideration is sleeping and resting quarters. Be sure to supply a dog bed for your pup, and introduce him to his special cozy corner so that he knows where to retire when he feels like taking a snooze. You'll need to buy a collar (or harness) and leash, a safe chew item (such as Nylabone® or Gumabone®), and a few grooming tools as well. A couple of sturdy feeding dishes, one for food and one for water, will be needed; and it will be necessary, beforehand, to set up a feeding station.

Chain-link fencing is a good, sturdy material to use for building dog runs and kennels.

canine diseases, and make certain you secure all health certificates at the time of purchase. This information will be valuable to your veterinarian, who will want to know the puppy's complete medical history. Incidentally, don't wait until your puppy becomes sick before you seek the services of a vet; make an appointment for your pup before or soon after he takes up residence with you so that he starts out with a clean bill of health in his new home.

FINDING A VETERINARIAN

An important part of your preparations should include finding a local veterinarian who can provide quality health care in the form of routine

CHILDREN AND PUPPIES

Prepare the young members of the household on pet care. Children should learn not only to love their charges but to respect them and treat them with the consideration one would give all living things. It must be emphasized to youngsters that the puppy has certain needs, just as humans have, and all family members must take an active role in ensuring that these needs are met. Someone must feed the puppy. Someone must walk him a couple of times a day or clean up after him if he is trained to relieve himself on newspaper. Someone must groom his coat, clean his ears, and clip his nails from time to time. Someone must see to it that the puppy gets sufficient exercise and squeezing and hugging the animal in ways which are irritating or even painful. Others have been found guilty of teasing, perhaps unintentionally, and disturbing their pet while the animal is eating or resting. One must teach a child, therefore, when and how to gently stroke and fondle a puppy. In time, the child can learn how to carefully pick up and handle the pup. A dog should always be supported with both hands, *not* lifted by the scruff of the neck. One hand placed under the chest, between the front legs, and the other hand supporting the dog's rear end

attention each day.

A child who has a pet to care for learns responsibility; nonetheless, parental guidance is an essential part of his learning experience. Many a child has been known to "love a pet to death,"

This famous show dog is Champion Merrimar Queen of the Nile, also known as "Cleo" to her friends. Owned by Mrs. William H. Ball, Cleo is pictured winning one of her numerous important wins, this one a Best of Variety.

will be comfortable and will restrain the animal as you hold and carry him. Always demonstrate to children the proper way to lift a dog.

BE A GOOD NEIGHBOR

For the sake of your dog's safety and well being, don't allow him to wander onto the property of others. Keep him confined at all times to your own yard or indoors where he won't become a nuisance. Consider what dangers lie ahead for an unleashed dog that has total freedom of the great outdoors, particularly when he is unsupervised by his master. There are cars and trucks to dodge on the streets and highways. There are stray animals with which to wrangle. There are poisons all around, such as car antifreeze in driveways or toxic plants and shrubs, which, if swallowed, could prove fatal. There are dognappers and sadistic people who may steal or bring harm to your beloved pet. In short, there are all sorts of nasty things waiting to hurt him. Did you know that if your dog consumes rotting garbage, there is the possibility he could go into shock or even die? And are you aware that a dog left to roam in a wooded area or field could become infected with any number of parasites if he plays with or ingests some small prey, such as a rabbit, that might be carrying these parasitic organisms? A thorn from a rosebush

Periodically your Poodle will need a bath. Make certain that you brush out all of the tangles and mats before you bathe him; otherwise, these will become hard to manage later on. Photo by Sally Anne Thompson.

imbedded in the dog's foot pad, tar from a newly paved road stuck to his coat, or a

45

wound inflicted by a wild animal all can be avoided if you take the precaution of keeping your dog in a safe enclosure where he will be protected from such dangers. Don't let your dog run loose; he is likely to stray from home and get into all sorts of trouble.

Many cities and towns now have ordinances that apply to keeping dogs as pets, and in a number of these municipalities there are animal control officials or dog wardens whose job it is to enforce these regulations. In fact, in certain areas there are fines imposed on dog owners who are negligent about controlling their animals. One such familiar regulation involves the curbing of dogs, for sanitary as well as esthetic reasons. In quite a few areas, dog owners are prohibited from allowing their canines, whether leashed or unleashed, to defecate or urinate on someone else's property. There are laws in most places which require dogs to be licensed and inoculated against the dread disease, rabies. Laws, of course, vary from place to place, so save yourself from legal headaches by finding out which rules in your

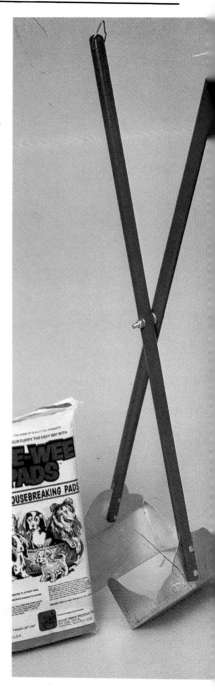

Housebreaking your dog can be made easier by using a "pooper scooper," a long-handled tool for picking up fecal matter outdoors or inside kennels and runs.

community apply to you as a dog owner. The laws, it should be mentioned, are designed not only to protect the citizenry from acts of canine destruction; they also serve as protection for your dog! So don't wait until your pooch accidentally mauls a young child or scatters the contents of your neighbor's

new environment. Avoid introducing the pup to the family around holiday time, since all of the extra excitement will only add to the confusion and frighten him. Let the puppy enter your home on a day when the routine is normal. For those people who work during the week, a Saturday morning is

Well-constructed dog houses should offer protection from the elements. This model has a "front porch" and the back room serves as the dog's sleeping quarters.

garbage cans or digs holes in carefully cultivated flower beds to exercise your responsibility. Start with a proper attitude as soon as your four-legged companion becomes part of your family.

GETTING ACQUAINTED

Plan to bring your new pet home in the morning so that by nightfall he will have had some time to become acquainted with you and his

an ideal time to bring the puppy to his new home; this way he has the entire weekend to make adjustments before being left alone for a few hours, come Monday morning.

Let the puppy explore, under your watchful eye of course, and let him come to know his new home without stress and fear. Resist the temptation to handle him too much during these first few days. And, if there are other dogs or animals around the house, make certain all are properly introduced. If you observe fighting among the

Poodles can also be trained to sit still for the more serious shots (top). Most people find that their dogs are extremely affectionate, as is the case with this white Standard, Champion Alekai Zeus (bottom).

animals, or some other problem, you may have to separate all parties until they learn to accept one another. Remember that neglecting your other pets while showering the new puppy with extra attention will only cause animosity and jealousy. Make an effort to pay special attention to the other animals as well.

On that eventful first night, try not to give in and let the puppy sleep with you; otherwise, this could become a difficult habit to break. Let him cry and whimper, even if it means a night of restlessness for the entire family. Some people have had success with putting a doll or a hot water bottle wrapped in a towel in the puppy's bed as a surrogate mother, while others have placed a ticking alarm clock in the bed to simulate the heartbeat of the pup's dam and littermates. Remember that this furry little fellow is used to the warmth and security of his mother and siblings, so the adjustment to sleeping alone will take time. Select a location away from drafts and away from the feeding station for placement of his dog bed. Keep in mind, also, that the bed should be roomy enough for him to stretch out in; as he grows older, you may need to supply a larger one.

Prior to the pup's arrival, set up his room and partition it the way you would to keep an infant out of a particular area. You may want to keep his bed, his feeding station, and his toilet area all in the same room—in separate locations—or you may want to set the feeding station up in your kitchen, perhaps, where meals for all family members are served. Whatever you decide, do it ahead of time so that you will have that much less to worry about when your puppy finally moves in with you.

Above all else, be patient with your puppy as he adjusts to life in his new home. If you purchased a pup that is not housebroken, you will have to spend time with the dog—just as you would with a small child—until he develops proper toilet habits. Even a housebroken puppy may feel nervous in strange new surroundings and have an occasional accident. Praise and encouragement will elicit

far better results than punishment or scolding. Remember that your puppy wants nothing more than to please you.

Dog breeders and owners come up with all sorts of interesting names for their animals; many are inspired by television and movie characters.

Feeding Requirements

Soon after your puppy comes to live with you, he will need to be fed. As mentioned already, ask the seller what foods were offered the youngster and stay with that diet for a while. It is important for the puppy to keep eating and to avoid skipping a meal, so entice him with the food to which he is accustomed. If you prefer to switch to some other brand of dog food, each day begin to add small quantities of the new brand to

relatively inexpensive to prepare. Puppies need to be fed small portions at frequent intervals, since they are growing and their activity level is high. You must ensure that your pup gains weight steadily; with an adult dog,

Food and water dishes need to be washed with soap and hot water and rinsed well each day. Select ones that are easy to clean and heavy so that they won't tip over.

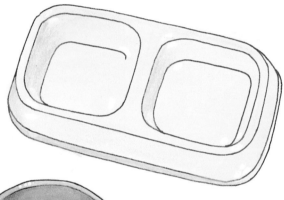

the usual food offering. Make the portions of the new food progressively larger until the pup is weaned from his former diet.

What should you feed the puppy and how often? His diet is really quite simple and

however, growth slows down and weight must be regulated to prevent obesity and a host of other problems. At one time it was thought that home-cooked meals were the answer, with daily rations of meat, vegetables, egg yolk, cereal, cheese, brewer's yeast, and vitamin supplements. With all of the nutritionally complete commercial dog food products readily available, these time-consuming preparations really are unnecessary now. A great deal of money and research

Dry food is convenient to store, easy to prepare, and it won't spoil easily. There are numerous dog foods from which to choose, ones that are nutritionally complete and balanced.

has resulted in foods that we can serve our dogs with confidence and pride; and most of these commercial foods have been developed along strict guidelines according to the size, weight, and age of your dog. These products are reasonably priced, easy to find, and convenient to store.

THE PUPPY'S MEALS

After a puppy has been fully weaned from its mother until approximately three months of age, it needs to be fed four times a day. In the morning and evening offer kibble (dog meal) soaked in hot water or broth, to which you have added some canned meat-based food or fresh raw meat cut into small chunks. At noon and bedtime feed him a bit of kibble or whole-grain cereal moistened with milk (moistening, by the way, makes the food easier to digest, since dogs don't typically chew their food). From three to six months, increase the portion size and offer just three meals—one milk and two meat. At six months, two meals are sufficient; at one year, a

A slicker brush is used on long-coated breeds, such as the Poodle, to remove mats and tangles. This should be done prior to bathing. Be especially careful as you work around such sensitive areas as the eyes, the ears, the nose, and the mouth.

single meal can be given, supplemented with a few dry biscuits in the morning and evening. During the colder months, especially if your dog is active, you might want to mix in some wheat germ oil or corn oil or bacon drippings with the meal to add extra calories. Remember to keep a bowl of cool, fresh water on hand always to help your dog regulate its body temperature and to aid in digestion.

From one year on, you may continue feeding the mature dog a single meal (in the evening, perhaps, when you have your supper), or you may prefer to divide this meal in two, offering half in the morning and the other half at

COMPARISON SHOPPING

With so many fine dog-food products on the market today, there is something for everyone's pet. You may want to serve dry food "as is" or mix it with warm water or broth. Perhaps you'll choose to combine dry food with fresh or canned preparations. Some canned foods contain

The toenails on this handsome Poodle have just been clipped. If your dog is allowed to walk and run on concrete surfaces, you probably won't have to clip the nails at all.

night. Keep in mind that while puppies require foods in small chunks, or nuggets, older dogs can handle larger pieces of food at mealtime. Discuss your dog's feeding schedule with your veterinarian; he can make suggestions about the right diet for your particular canine friend.

all meat, but they are not complete; others are mixtures of meat and grains, which have been fortified with additional nutrients to make them complete and balanced. There are also various packaged foods that can be served alone or as supplements and that can be left out for a few hours without spoiling. This self-feeding method, which works well for dogs that are not prone to overweight problems, allows the animal to serve himself whenever he feels hungry. Many people who work during the day find these dry or semi-moist rations convenient to use, and these foods are great to bring along if you travel with your dog.

Be sure to read the labels carefully before you make your dog-food purchases. Most reputable pet-food manufacturers list the ingredients and the nutritional content right on the can or package. Instructions are usually included, besides, so that you will know how much to feed your dog to keep him thriving and in top condition. A varied, well-balanced diet that supplies the proper amounts of protein, carbohydrate, fat, vitamins, minerals, and water is important to keep your puppy healthy and to guarantee its normal development. Adjustments to the diet can

Hard food morsels, or kibble, help keep tartar from building up on your dog's teeth. This convenient dry food can be left out for self-feeding. Photo courtesy of Nutro Products, Inc.

be made, under your veterinarian's supervision, according to the individual puppy, his rate of growth, his activity level, and so on. Liquid or powder vitamin and mineral supplements, or those in tablet form, are available and can be given if you need to feel certain that the diet is balanced.

DEVELOPING GOOD EATING HABITS

Try to serve your puppy its meals at the same time each day and in the same location so that he will get used to his daily routine and develop good eating habits. A bit of raw egg, cottage cheese, or table scraps (leftover food from your own meals) can be offered from time to time; but never accustom your dog to eating human "junk food." Cake, candy, chocolate, soda, and other snack foods are for people, not dogs. Besides, these foods provide only "empty" calories that your pet doesn't need if he is to stay healthy. Avoid offering spicy, fried, fatty, or starchy foods, rather, offer leftover meats, vegetables, and gravies. Get in the habit of feeding your puppy or your grown dog his *own* daily meals of dog food. If ever you are in doubt about what foods and how much to serve, consult your veterinarian.

ALL DOGS NEED TO CHEW

Puppies and young dogs need something with

Automatic waterers are convenient to use and provide a constant water supply for your dog.

resistance to chew on while their teeth and jaws are developing—for cutting the puppy teeth, to induce growth of the permanent teeth under the puppy teeth, to assist in getting rid of the puppy teeth at the proper time, to help the permanent teeth through the gums, to assure normal jaw development and to settle the permanent teeth solidly in the jaws.

The adult dog's desire to chew stems from the instinct for tooth cleaning, gum massage and jaw exercise—plus the need to vent periodic

55

doggie tensions.

Dental caries, as it affects the teeth of humans, is virtually unknown in dogs; but tartar accumulates on the teeth of dogs, particularly at the gum line, more rapidly than on the teeth of humans. These accumulations, if not removed, bring irritation and then infection, which erodes the tooth enamel and ultimately destroys the teeth at the roots.

Tooth and jaw development will normally continue until the

These pups (top) soon will be weaned from their mother as their tiny teeth start to push through the gums. To help the puppies through their teething stage, ask your local pet shop to recommend an appropriate chew product manufactured by the Nylabone® Corporation. A gorgeous apricot Miniature bitch, Champion Tiopepi Amber Tanya (bottom), imported from England by Mrs. Gardner Cassatt of Beaufresne Miniature Poodles.

dog is more than a year old—but sometimes much longer, depending upon the dog, chewing exercise, the rate at which calcium can be utilized and many other factors, known and unknown, which affect the development of individual dogs. Diseases, like distemper for example, may sometimes arrest development of the teeth and jaws, which may resume months or even years later.

This is why dogs, especially puppies and young dogs, will

Gumabone® is the safest chew toy that you can give your dog— it's proven to be safer and lasts at least ten times longer than similar products made of rawhide, rubber, or vinyl. When the Gumabone® wears down, as indicated in this photo, simply replace it with a new one.

often destroy valuable property when their chewing instinct is not diverted from their owner's possessions, particularly during the widely varying critical period for young dogs. Saving your possessions from destruction, assuring proper development of teeth and jaws, providing for "interim" tooth cleaning and gum massage, and channeling doggie tensions into a non-destructive outlet are, therefore, all dependent upon the dog's having something suitable for chewing readily available

when his instinct tells him to chew. If your purposes, and those of your dog, are to be accomplished, what you provide for chewing must be desirable from the doggie viewpoint, have the necessary functional qualities, and, above all, be safe for your dog.

It is very important that dogs not be permitted to chew on anything they can break or indigestible things from which they can bite sizeable chunks. Sharp pieces, such as those from a bone which can be broken by a dog, may pierce the intestine wall and kill. Indigestible things which can be bitten off in chunks, such as toys made of rubber compound or cheap plastic, may cause an intestinal stoppage; if not regurgitated, they are certain to bring painful death unless surgery is promptly performed.

Strong natural bones, such

Nylabone® products come in a variety of shapes, sizes, and flavors to suit every dog's taste. Since these therapeutic devices help cleanse your dog's teeth and massage his gums, they are highly recommended by veterinarians.

as 4 to 8 inch lengths of round shin bone from mature beef—either the kind you can get from your butcher or one of the varieties available commercially in pet stores—may serve your dog's teething needs, if his mouth is large enough to handle them effectively.

You may be tempted to give your puppy a smaller bone and he may not be able to break it when you do, but puppies grow rapidly and the power of their jaws constantly increases until maturity. This means that a growing dog

may break one of the smaller bones at any time, swallow the pieces and die painfully before you realize what is wrong.

Many people have the mistaken notion that their dog's teeth are like those of wild carnivores or of dogs from antiquity. The teeth of wild carnivorous animals and those found in the fossils of the dog-like creatures of antiquity have far thicker and stronger enamel than those of our contemporary dogs.

All hard, natural bones are highly abrasive. If your dog is an avid chewer, natural bones may wear away his teeth prematurely; hence, they then

Pet shops sell entire lines of dog-food products that are complete and nutritionally balanced. Photo courtesy of Nutro Products, Inc.

should be taken away from your dog when the teething purposes have been served. The badly worn, and usually painful, teeth of many mature dogs can be traced to excessive chewing on animal bones. Contrary to popular belief, knuckle bones that can be chewed up and swallowed by the dog provide little, if any, useable calcium or other nutriment. They do, however, disturb the digestion of most dogs and might cause them to vomit the nourishing food they really need.

Never give a dog your old shoe to chew on, even if you have removed all the nails or metal parts, such as lace grommets, buckles, metal arches, and so on. Rubber heels are especially dangerous, as the dog can bite off chunks, swallow them,

ALL DOGS NEED TO CHEW

and suffer from intestinal blockage as a result. Additionally, if the rubber should happen to have a nail imbedded in it that you cannot detect, this could pierce or tear the intestinal wall. There is always the possibility, too, that your dog may fail to differentiate between his shoe and yours and chew up a good pair while you're not looking. It is strongly recommended that you refrain from offering old shoes as chew toys since there are much safer products available.

Rawhide products have become very popular. However they don't serve the primary chewing functions very well, they are a bit messy when wet from mouthing, and most dogs chew them up rather rapidly. They have been considered safe for dogs until recently. Now, more and more incidents of death, and near death, by strangulation have been reported to be the result of partially swallowed chunks of rawhide swelling in the throat. Currently, some veterinarians have been attributing cases of acute constipation to large pieces of incompletely digested rawhide in the intestine.

The nylon bones, especially those with natural meat and bone fractions added, are probably the most complete, safe and economical answer to the chewing need. Dogs cannot break them or bite off sizeable chunks; hence, they

are completely safe. And being longer lasting than other things offered for the purpose, they are economical.

Hard chewing raises little bristle-like projections on the surface of the nylon bones to provide effective interim tooth cleaning and vigorous gum massage, much in the same way your tooth brush does it for you. The little projections are raked off and swallowed in the form of thin shavings, but the chemistry of the nylon is such that they break down in the stomach fluids and pass through without effect.

The toughness of the nylon provides the strong chewing resistance needed for important jaw exercise and effective help for the teething functions; however, there is no tooth wear because nylon is non-abrasive. Being inert, nylon does not support the growth of microorganisms; and it can be washed in soap and water, or it can be sterilized by boiling or in an autoclave.

There are a great variety of Nylabone® products available that veterinarians recommend as safe and healthy for your dog or puppy to chew on. These Nylabone® Pooch Pacifiers® can't splinter, chip, or break off in large chunks; instead, they are frizzled by the dog's chewing action, and this creates a toothbrush-like surface that cleanses the teeth and massages the gums. At the same time, these hard-nylon therapeutic devices channel doggie tension and chewing frustation into constructive rather than destructive behavior. Unfortunately, many nylon chew products have been copied. These inferior quality copies are sold in supermarkets and other chain stores. The really good products are sold only through veterinarians, pet shops, grooming salons and places where the sales people really know something about dogs. The good products have the flavor impregnated INTO the bone. This makes the taste last longer. The smell is undetectable to humans. The artificial bones which have a strong odor are poor-quality bones with the odor sprayed on to impress the dog owner (not the dog)! These heavily scented dog toys may impart the odor to your carpets or furniture if an odor-sprayed bone lies there wet from a dog's chewing on it.

If you want a soft, chewy play toy, look for Gumabone® products wherever Nylabone® products are sold. These flexible toys are available in various sizes of bones, balls, knots, and rings (and even a tug toy) designed to provide safe entertainment for you and your dog. These great aids for teaching your canine companion how to retrieve are made of a soft, thermoplastic polymer that lasts at least ten times longer than other rawhide, rubber, or vinyl chew toys, making them

very economical. If your dog is able to chew apart a Gumabone® toy, although most dogs cannot, it is probably because you gave him a Gumabone® toy that was too small. Replace it with a larger one and most likely he will not be able to chew it

The eyerims, lips, nose, and toenails should be black in black Poodles. Additionally, the coat should be a deep, intense, glowing black that, in the sun, gives off an almost metallic blue-black tone.

apart. These ham-flavored toys will provide scores of hours of fun for most dogs that like chewing on soft items.

Nothing, however, substitutes for periodic professional attention to your dog's teeth and gums, not any more than your toothbrush can do that for you. Have your dog's teeth cleaned by your

With the addition of Gumabone® to the arsenal of dog chew toys, petshops are now offering better quality chew toys. It is of the utmost importance that the size of the Gumabone® match the size of the dog. A large dog can chew through, or swallow, a toy too small for it. The great advantage of Nylabone® and Gumabone® is that they are made by a company who ONLY makes dog toys and therapeutic devices. They usually guarantee that their products will last much longer than any chain store or supermarket copy and they will replace the Gumabone® with a larger size, free of charge, if your dog chews it up very quickly. It is normal for a dog to chew on the knuckle. The bone shown above is ready to be replaced, since the knuckle has been chewed down on one end. The small particles of Nylabone® and Gumabone® that the dog chews off normally pass through the digestive tract as roughage.

veterinarian at least once a year—twice a year is better—and he will be healthier, happier and a far more pleasant companion.

FEEDING GUIDELINES

Some things to bear in mind with regard to your dog's feeding regimen follow:

- Nutritional balance, provided by many commercial dog foods, is vital; avoid feeding a one-sided diet of all-meat. Variety in the kinds of meat (beef, lamb, chicken, liver) or cereal grains (wheat, oats, corn) that you offer your dog is of secondary importance compared to the balance or "completeness" of dietary components.

- Always refrigerate opened canned food so that it doesn't

Chocolate-flavored and ham-scented Nylabones® are real favorites with dogs. Incidentally, in the former the thin film of chocolate is just beneath the surface where it can't be washed off or licked off.

spoil. Remember to remove all uneaten portions of canned or moistened food from the feeding dish as soon as the pup has finished his meal. Discard the leftover food immediately and thoroughly wash and dry the

should be made available at all times, incidentally, even if dry foods are not left out for self-feeding. Each day the water dish should be washed in soap and hot water, rinsed well, and dried; a refill of clean, fresh water should be provided daily.

● Food and water should be served at room temperature, neither too hot nor too cold, so that it is more palatable for your puppy.

● Serve your pup's meals in sturdy hard-plastic, stainless steel, or earthenware containers, ones that won't tip over as the dog bolts his food down. Some bowls and dishes are weighted to prevent spillage, while others fit neatly into holders which offer support. Feeding dishes should be large enough to hold each meal.

● Whenever the nutritional needs of your dog change, that is to say, when it grows old; if it becomes ill, obese, or pregnant; or if it starts to nurse its young, special diets are in order. Always contact your vet for advice on these special dietary requirements.

● Feed your puppy at the same regular intervals each day; reserve treats for special occasions or, perhaps, to reward good behavior during training sessions.

This Poodle is enjoying the outdoors under the watchful eye of his owner. Never allow your dog to roam around outside, even on your own property, without being there to supervise.

feeding dish, as dirty dishes are a breeding ground for harmful germs.

● When offering dry foods, always keep a supply of water on hand for your dog. Water

Accommodations

Puppies newly weaned from their mother and siblings should be kept warm at all times. As they get older, gradually they can be acclimated to cooler temperatures. When you purchase your dog, find out from the seller whether he is hardy and can withstand the rigors of outdoor living. Many breeds have been known to adapt well to a surprising number of environments, so long as they are given time to adjust. If your pup is to be an indoor companion, perhaps a dog bed in the corner of the family room will suffice, or maybe you'll want to invest in a crate for him to call his "home" whenever he needs to be confined for short intervals. You might plan to partition off a special room, or part of a room, for your pooch; or you may find that a heated garage or finished basement works well as your dog's living quarters. If your

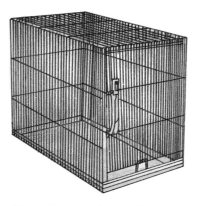

Never allow your dog to ride in the car unconfined; always place him in a crate to ensure his safety.

breed can tolerate living outside, you may want to buy or build him his own dog house with an attached run. Or it might be feasible to place his house in your fenced-in backyard. The breed that can live outdoors fares well when he has access to some sort of warm, dry shelter during periods of inclement weather. As you begin thinking about where your canine friend will spend most of his time, you'll want to consider his breed, his age, his temperament, his need for exercise, and the money, space, and resources you have available to house him.

THE DOG BED

In preparing for your puppy's arrival, it is recommended that a dog bed be waiting for him so that he has a place to sleep and rest. If indeed you have provided him with his own bed or

Portable exercise pens are useful whenever you travel with your dog.

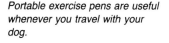
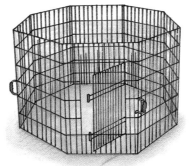

basket, ensure that it is in a warm, dry, draft-free spot that is private but at the same time near the center of family activity. Refrain from placing his bed near the feed and water dishes or his toilet area. You may want to give your puppy something with which to snuggle, such as a laundered towel or blanket or an article of old clothing. Some dogs have been known to chew apart their beds and

Every dog should have a bed of its own. Check your local pet shop for dog beds and other products that you will need to keep your dog healthy and happy.

roomy, comfortable, and easy to clean, keeping in mind that you may have to replace the smaller bed with a larger one as the puppy grows to adulthood. Remember to clean and disinfect the bed and sleeping area from time to time, as these can become parasitic playgrounds for fleas, lice, mites and the like.

THE CRATE

Although many dog lovers may cringe at the mere mention of the word *crate*, thinking of it as a cage or a

cruel means of confinement, this handy piece of equipment can be put to good use for puppies and grown dogs alike. Even though you may love your dog to an extraordinary degree, you may not want him to have free rein of the house, particularly when you are not home to supervise him. If used properly, a crate can restrict your dog when it is not

bedding, but you can easily channel this chewing energy into more constructive behavior simply by supplying him with some safe toys or a Nylabone® pacifier for gnawing. Pet shops stock dog beds, among other supplies that you might need for your pup; so select one that is

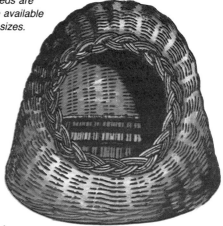

An alternative to dog beds are baskets, and these are available in various shapes and sizes.

convenient to have him underfoot, *i.e.,* when guests are visiting or during your mealtimes.

A surprising number of dog owners who, originally, had negative feelings about crating their dogs, have had great success using them. The crate itself serves as a bed, provided it is furnished with bedding material, or it can be used as an indoor dog house. Not all dogs readily accept crates or to being confined in them for short intervals, so for them another means of restriction must be found. But for those dogs that do adjust to spending time in these structures, the crate can be useful in many ways. The animal can be confined for a few hours while you are away from home or at work, or you can bring your crated dog along with you in the car when you travel or go on vacation. They also prove handy as carriers whenever you have to transport a sick dog to the veterinarian.

Most crates are made of sturdy wire or plastic and some of the collapsible models can be stored conveniently or folded so that they can be moved easily from room to room or from inside the house to the yard on a warm, sunny day. If you allow your puppy or grown dog to become acquainted with its crate by cleverly propping the door open and leaving some of his favorite toys inside, in no time he will come to regard the crate as his own doggie haven. As with a dog bed, place the crate away from drafts in a dry, warm spot; refrain from placing food and water dishes in it, as these only crowd the space and offer opportunity for spillage.

If you need to confine your puppy so that he can't get into mischief while you're not home, remember to consider the animal's needs at all times. Therefore, select a large crate, one in which the dog can stand up and move around comfortably; in fact, bigger is better in this context. Never leave the animal confined for more than a few hours at a time without letting him out to exercise, play, and, if necessary, relieve himself. Never crate a dog for ten hours, for example, unless you keep the door to the crate open so that he can get out for food and water and to stretch a bit. If long intervals of confinement are necessary, consider placing the unlatched crate in a partitioned section of your house or apartment.

Crates have become the answer for many a dog owner faced with the dilemma of either getting rid of a destructive dog or living with him despite his bad habits. These people who have neither the time nor the patience to train their dogs, or to modify undesirable behavior patterns, can at least restrain their pets during those times they can't be there to supervise. So long as the crate is used in a humane fashion, whereby a dog is

confined for no more than a few hours at any one time, it can figure importantly in a dog owner's life. Show dogs, incidentally, learn at an early age that much time will be spent in and out of crates while they are on the show circuit. Many canine celebrities are kept in their crates until they are called to ringside, and they spend many hours crated to and from the shows.

THE DOG HOUSE

These structures, often made of wood, should be made sturdily and offer enough room for your dog to

There is no need to build your dog his own house when there are commercially-made ones from which to choose.

stretch out in when it rests or sleeps. Dog houses that are elevated or situated on a platform protect the animal from cold and dampness that may seep through the ground. Of the breeds that are temperature hardy and will live outdoors, some are housed outside during the daytime only; others are permanent outdoor residents day and night, all year 'round.

If your intention is to have a companion that lives out-of-doors, it will be necessary to provide him with a more elaborate house, one that really protects from him the elements. Make sure the dog's house is constructed of waterproof materials. Furnish him with sufficient bedding to burrow into on a chilly night and provide extra insulation to keep out drafts and wet weather. Add a partition (a kind of room divider which separates the entry area from the main sleeping space) inside his house or attach a swinging door to the entrance to help keep him warm when he is inside his residence. The swinging door facilitates entry to and from the dog house, while at the same time it provides protection, particularly from wind and drafts.

This traditional style dog house is made of non-toxic polymer, which keeps your dog cool in summer and warm in winter; additionally, it is strong, durable, and easy to clean.

Some fortunate owners whose yards are enclosed by high fencing allow their dogs complete freedom within the boundaries of their property. In these situations, a dog can leave its dog house and get all the exercise it wants. Of course such a large space requires more effort to keep clean. An alternative to complete backyard freedom is a dog kennel or run which attaches to or surrounds the dog's house. This restricts some forms of movement, such as running, perhaps, but it does provide ample room for walking, climbing, jumping, and stretching. Another option is to fence off part of the yard and place the dog house in the enclosure. If you need to tether your dog to its house, make certain to use a fairly long lead so as not to

hamper the animal's need to move and exercise his limbs.

CLEANLINESS

No matter where your dog lives, either in or out of your home, be sure to keep him in surroundings as clean and sanitary as possible. His excrement should be removed and disposed of every day without fail. No dog should be forced to lie in his own feces. If your dog lives in his own house, the floor should be

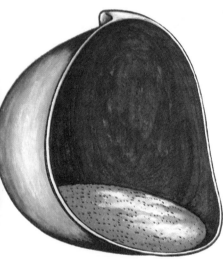

The dome-like dog bed— a real doggie haven —features a soft, furry cushion for your dog's comfort.

swept occasionally and the bedding should be changed regularly if it becomes soiled. Food and water dishes need to be scrubbed with hot water and detergent and rinsed well to remove all traces of soap.

The water dish should be refilled with a supply of fresh water. The dog and his environment must be kept free of parasites (especially fleas and mosquitoes, which can carry disease) with products designed to keep these pests under control. Dog crates need frequent scrubbing, too, as do the floors of kennels and runs. Your pet must be kept clean and comfortable at all times; if you exercise strict sanitary control, you will keep disease and parasite infestation to a minimum.

EXERCISE

A well-balanced diet and regular medical attention from a qualified veterinarian are essential in promoting good health for your dog, but so is daily exercise to keep him fit and mentally alert. Dogs that have been confined all day while their owners are at work or school need special attention. There should be some time set aside each day for play—a romp with a family member, perhaps. Not everyone is lucky enough to let his dog run through an open meadow or along a sandy beach, but even a ten-minute walk in the fresh air will do. Dogs that are house-bound, particularly those that live in apartments, need to be walked out-of-doors after each meal so that they can relieve themselves. Owners can make this daily ritual more pleasant both for themselves and their canine companions by combining the walk with a little "roughhousing," that is to say, a bit of fun and togetherness.

Whenever possible, take a stoll to an empty lot, a playground, or a nearby park. Attach a long lead to your dog's collar, and let him run and jump and tone his body through cardiovascular activity. This will help him burn calories and keep him trim, but it will also help relieve tension and stress that may have had a chance to manifest itself while you were away all day. For people who work Monday through Friday, weekend jaunts can be especially beneficial, since there will be more time to spend with your canine friend. You might want to engage him in a simple game of fetch with a stick or a rubber ball. Even such basic tricks as rolling over, standing on the hindlegs, or jumping up (all of which can be done inside the home as well) can provide additional exercise. But if you plan to challenge your dog with a real workout to raise his heart rate, remember not to push him too hard without first warming up with a brisk walk. Don't forget to "cool him down" afterwards with a

Your dog needs regular exercise, and one way to provide this is to toss a flying disc to him a number of times so that he gets a good workout.

rhythmic trot until his heart rate returns to normal. Some dog owners jog with their dogs or take them along on bicycle excursions.

The skeleton of Canis familiaris *is similar to that of most mammals, including man.*

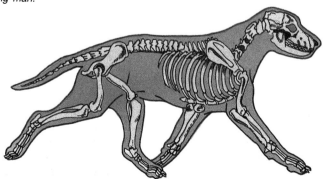

Housebreaking Your Puppy

The new addition to your family may already have received some basic house training before his arrival in your home. If he has not, remember that a puppy will want to relieve himself about half a dozen times a day; it is up to you to specify where and when he should "do his business." Housebreaking is your first training concern and should begin the moment you bring the puppy home.

There are all sorts of brushes made for grooming dogs; ask your local pet shop for the one that will keep your dog's coat looking its best.

Ideally, puppies should be taken outdoors after meals, as a full stomach will exert pressure on the bladder and colon. What goes into the dog must eventually come out; the period after his meal is the most natural and appropriate time. When he eliminates, he should be praised and this will increase the likelihood of the same thing happening after every meal. He should also be encouraged to use the same area and will probably be attracted to it after frequent use.

OUTDOOR TRAINING

Some veterinarians have maintained that a puppy could learn to urinate and defecate on command if properly trained. The advantage of this conditioning technique is that your pet would associate the act of elimination with a particular word of your invention rather than with a particular time or place which might not always be convenient or available. So whether you were visiting an unfamiliar place or didn't want to go outside with your dog in sub-zero temperatures, he would still be able to relieve himself when he heard the specific command word. Elimination would occur after this "trigger" phrase or word had set up a conditioned reflex in the dog who would eliminate anything contained in his bladder or bowel upon hearing it. The shorter the word, the more you could repeat it and imprint it on your dog's memory.

Your chosen command word should be given simultaneously with the sphincter opening events in order to achieve perfect and rapid conditioning. This is why it is important initially to familiarize yourself with the tell-tale signs preceding your puppy's elimination process. Then you will be prepared to say the word at the crucial moment. There is usually a sense of urgency on the dog's part; he may follow a sniffing and circling pattern which you will soon recognize. It is important to use the command in his usual area only when you know the puppy can eliminate, *i.e.*, when his stomach or bladder is full. He will soon learn to associate the act with the word. One word of advice, however, if you plan to try out this method: never use the puppy's name or any other word which he might frequently hear about the house—you can imagine the result!

Finally, remember that any training takes time. Such a conditioned response can be obtained with intensive practice with any normal, healthy dog over six weeks of age. Even Pavlov's salivating dogs required fifty repetitions before the desired response was achieved. Patience and

cover the specific area where your dog should relieve himself. These should be placed some distance away from his sleeping and feeding area, as a puppy will not urinate or defecate where he eats. When the newspapers are changed, the bottom papers should be placed on top of the new ones in order to evoke the purpose of the papers by scent as well as by sight. He should be praised during or immediately after he has made use of this particular part of the room. Each positive reinforcement increases the possibility of his using that area again.

When he arrives, it is advisable to limit the puppy to

The so-called "pooper scooper" is handy for picking up after your dog. It is especially useful in areas that require you to curb your dog.

persistence will eventually produce results—do not lose heart!

INDOOR TRAINING

Indoors, sheets of newspapers could be used to

one room, usually the kitchen, as it most likely has a linoleum or easily washable floor surface. Given the run of the house, the sheer size of the place will seem overwhelming and confusing and he might leave his "signature" on your furniture or clothes! There will be time later to familiarize him gradually with his new surroundings.

PATIENCE, PERSISTENCE, AND PRAISE

As with a human baby, you must be patient, tolerant, and understanding of your pet's mistakes, making him feel loved and wanted, not rejected and isolated. You wouldn't hit a baby for soiling his diapers as you would realize that he was not yet able to control his bowel movements; be as compassionate with your canine infant. Never rub his nose in his excreta. Never indulge in the common practice of punishing him with a rolled-up newspaper. Never hit a puppy with your hand. He will only become "hand-shy" and learn to fear you. Usually the punishment is meted out sometime after the offense so it loses its efficacy anyway as the bewildered dog cannot connect the two events. Moreover, by association, he will soon learn

to be afraid of you and anything to do with newspapers—including, perhaps, that area where he is *supposed* to relieve himself!

Most puppies are eager to please; praise, encourgement, and reward (particularly the food variety) will produce far better results than any scolding or physical punishment. Moreover, it is far better to dissuade your puppy from doing certain things, like chewing on chair legs or other furniture, by making those objects particularly distasteful to him. You could smear them with a generous amount of hot chili sauce or cayenne pepper mixed with petroleum jelly, for example. This would make it

Plan to stock up on newspaper for housebreaking your puppy.

74

seem as if the object itself was administering the punishment whenever he attempted to chew it. He probably wouldn't need a second reminder!

Remember that the reason a dog has housebreaking or behavior problems is because his owner has allowed them to develop. This is why you must begin as you intend to continue, by letting your dog know what is acceptable and unacceptable behavior. It is also important that you be consistent in your demands; you cannot feed him from the dining room table one day and then punish him when he begs for food from your dinner guests.

TRAINING IS NECESSARY

You will want the newest member of your family to be welcomed by everyone; this will not happen if he urinates in every room of the house or barks all night! He needs training in the correct forms of behavior in this new, human world and you cannot expect your puppy to become the perfect pet overnight. He needs your help in his socialization process. Training greatly facilitates and enhances the relationship of the dog to his owner and to

the rest of society. A successfully trained dog can be taken anywhere and behave well with anyone. Indeed, it is that one crucial word—*training*—which can transform an aggressive animal into a peaceful, well-behaved pet. Now, how does this "transformation" take place?

WHEN AND HOW TO TRAIN

Like housebreaking, training should begin as soon as the puppy enters the house. The formal training sessions should be short but frequent, for example, ten to fifteen minute periods three times a day. These are much more effective than long, tiring sessions of half an hour which might soon become boring.

THE COLLAR AND LEACH

Your puppy should become used to a collar and leash as soon as possible. If he is very young, a thin, choke-chain collar could be used, but you will need a larger and heavier one for training when he is a little older. Remember to have his name and address on an identification tag attached to his collar, as you don't want to lose your pet if he should happen to leave your premises and explore the neighborhood!

Let the puppy wear his collar until he is used to how it feels. After a short time he will soon become accustomed to it and you can attach the leash. He might resist your

Some dog owners prefer to use the figure-eight–style harness instead of a collar.

You are building your relationship with your puppy during these times so make them as enjoyable as possible. It is a good idea to have these sessions *before* the puppy's meal, not after it when he wouldn't feel like exerting himself; the dog will then associate something pleasurable with his training sessions and look forward to them.

attempts to lead him or simply sit down and refuse to budge. Fight him for a few minutes, tugging on the leash if necessary, then let him relax for the day. He won't be trained until he learns that he must obey the pull under any circumstance, but this will take a few sessions. Remember that a dog's period of concentration is short, so little and often is the

Nylon-web dog collars have become quite popular and they can be found in a variety of attractive colors.

wisest course of action—and patience is the password to success.

GIVING COMMANDS

When you begin giving your puppy simple commands, make them as short as possible and use the same word with the same meaning at all times, for example, "Heel," "Sit," and "Stay." You must be consistent; otherwise your puppy will become confused. The dog's name should prefix all commands to attract his attention. Do not become impatient with him however many times you have to repeat your command.

A good way to introduce the "Come" command is by calling the puppy when his meal is ready. Once this has been learned, you could call your pet to you at will, always remembering to praise him for his prompt obedience. This "reward" or positive reinforcement is such a crucial part of training that a Director of the New York Academy of Dog Training constructed his whole

A six-foot training lead is a valuable piece of equipment to have on hand when you begin to train your dog.

teaching program upon the methods of "Love, Praise and Reward." Incidentally, if you use the command "Come," use it every time. Don't switch to "Come here" or "Come boy," as this will only confuse your dog.

exercise before his meal. After about five minutes, call him to you, praise him when he arrives, and slip his collar on him. Hold the leash tightly in your right hand; this should force the dog's head up and focus his attention on you. As

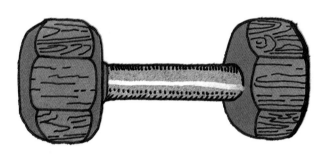

If you plan to enter your dog in obedience competition, one exercise he will have to master is the retrieving of a dumbbell.

It is worth underlining the fact that punishment is an ineffective teaching technique. We have already seen this in housebreaking and, for example, if your pup should run away, it would be senseless to beat him when he eventually returns. He would only connect the punishment with his return, not with the running away! Also, never call him to you to punish him, as he will soon learn not to respond when you call his name.

SOME SPECIFIC COMMANDS

"Sit." This is one of the easiest and most useful commands for your dog to learn, so it is a good idea to begin with it. The only equipment required is a leash, collar, and a few tasty tidbits. Take your dog out for some

you say "Sit" in a loud, clear voice, with your left hand press steadily on his rump until he is in a sitting position. As soon as he is in the correct position, praise him and give him the tidbit you have in your hand. Now wait a few minutes to let him rest and repeat the routine. Through repetition, the dog soon associates the word with the act. Never make the lesson too long. Eventually your praise will be reward enough for your puppy.

"Sit-Stay/Stay." To teach your pet to remain in one place or "stay" on your command, first of all order him to the sitting position at your side. Lower your left hand with the flat of your palm in front of his nose and your fingers pointing downwards. Hold the leash high and taut behind his head so that he cannot move. Speak the command "Sit-stay" and, as you are giving it, step in front of him. Repeat the command and tighten the leash so the animal cannot follow you. Walk completely around him, repeating the command and keeping him motionless by holding the leash at arm's length above him to check his

nylon cord or rope about twenty to thirty feet long. Repeat the whole routine from the beginning and be ready to prevent any movement towards you with a sharp "Sit-stay." Move around him in ever-widening circles until you are about fifteen feet away from him. If he still remains seated, you can pat yourself on the back! One useful thing

Another activity at obedience trials involves the dog's retrieving and leaping over the high jump.

movement. When he remains in this position for about fifteen seconds, you can begin the second part of the training. You will have to exchange the leash for a

to remember is that the dog makes associations with what you say, how you say it, and what you do while you are saying it. Do give this command in a firm, clear tone of voice, perhaps using an admonishing forefinger raised in warning to the dog to "stay."

TEACHING TO "HEEL," "COME" AND "DOWN"

When you walk your dog, you should hold the leash firmly in your right hand. The dog should walk on your left so you have the leash crossing your body. This enables you to have greater control over the dog.

Let your dog lead you for the first few moments so that he fully understands that freedom can be his if he goes about it properly. He knows already that when he wants to go outdoors the leash and collar are necessary, so he has respect for the leash. Now, if while walking he starts to pull in one direction, all you do is *stop walking.* He will walk a few steps and then find that he can't walk any further. He will then turn and look into your face. *This is the crucial point!* Just stand there for a moment and stare right back at him . . . now walk another ten feet and stop again. Again your dog will probably walk out the leash, find he can't go any further, and turn around and look again. If he starts to pull and jerk, then just stand there. After he quiets down, just bend down and comfort him as he may be frightened. Keep up this training until he learns not to outwalk you.

"Heel." Once the puppy obeys the pull of the leash,

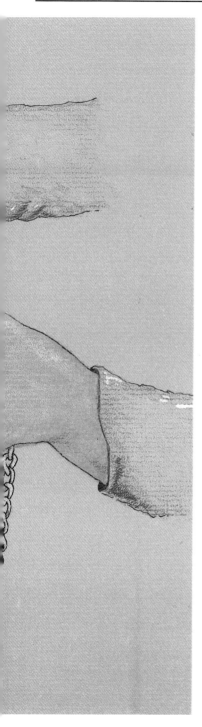

This is the correct way to place a choke chain on your dog. When placed correctly around the dog's neck, the chain should slacken when there is no pressure exerted from the lead attached to the collar.

half of your training is accomplished. "Heeling" is a necessity for a well-behaved dog, so teach him to walk beside you, head even with your knee. Nothing looks sadder than a big dog taking his helpless owner for a walk. It is annoying to passers-by and other dog owners to have a large dog, however friendly, bear down on them and entangle dogs, people, and packages.

To teach your dog, start off walking briskly, saying "Heel" in a firm voice. Pull back with a sharp jerk if he lunges ahead, and if he lags repeat the command and tug on the leash, not allowing him to drag behind. After the dog has learned to heel at various speeds on leash, you can remove it and practice heeling free, but have it ready to snap on again as soon as he wanders.

"Come." Your dog has already learned to come to you when you call his name. Why? Because you only call him when his food is ready or when you wish to play with him or praise him. Outdoors such a response is more difficult to achieve as he is happily playing by himself or with other dogs. So he must be trained to come to you when he is called. To teach him to come, let him reach the end of a long lead, then give the command, gently pulling him towards you at the same time. As soon as he associates the word *come* with the action of moving toward you, pull only when he does not respond immediately. As he starts to come, move back to make him learn that he must come from a distance as well as when he is close to you. Soon you may be able to practice without a leash, but if he is slow to come or actively disobedient, go to him and pull him toward you, repeating the command. Always remember to reward his successful completion of a task.

"Down." A puppy is naturally affectionate and excitable. However, not everyone likes to have a playful pup pounce on them with muddy paws or enthusiastically jump up to greet them. It is important that your puppy understands the command, "Down," and it should be one of the first lessons you teach.

One successful teaching strategy is to raise your knee and bump the dog in the stomach as he jumps up; you use this maneuver when puppies rush at you and leap at your chest. Or you could take him by his front legs and move him backward across the floor until he loses his balance and falls over. It will take patience and persistence before he gets the message but you will avoid a lot of dirty clothes and irate neighbors if you persevere!

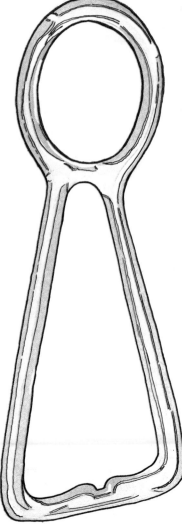

With this Gumabone® tug toy, manufactured by the Nylabone Corporation, you and your canine companion can get some real exercise!

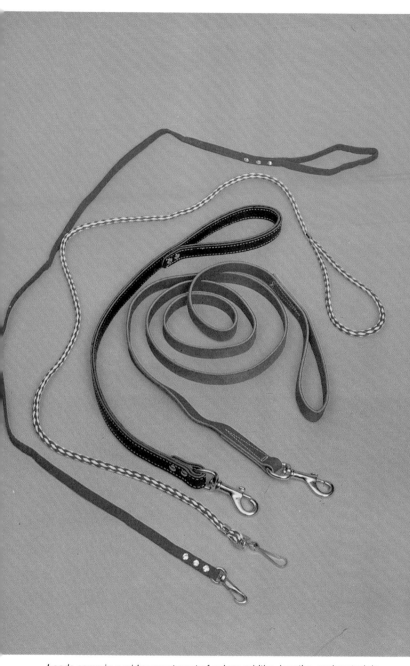

Leads come in a wide assortment of colors, widths, lengths, and materials. What is most important is that the lead you use be strong enough to hold the weight of your dog.

From the moment you purchase your puppy, the most important person in both your lives becomes your veterinarian. His professional advice and treatment will ensure the good health of your pet and he is the first person to call when illness or accidents occur. Do *not* try to be your own veterinarian or apply human remedies to canine diseases.

However, just as you would keep a first aid kit handy for minor injuries sustained by members of your family at home, so you should keep a similar kit prepared for your pet. First aid for your dog would consist of stopping any bleeding, cleaning the wound, and preventing infection. Thus your kit might contain medicated powder, gauze bandages, and adhesive tape to be used in case of cuts. If the cut is deep and bleeding profusely, the bandage should be applied very tightly to help in the formation of a clot. A tight bandage should not be kept in place longer than necessary, so take your pet to the veterinarian immediately.

Walking or running on a cut pad prevents the cut from healing. Proper suturing of the cut and regular changing of the bandages should have your pet's wound healed in a week to ten days. A minor cut should be covered with a light bandage, for you want as much air as possible to reach the wound. Do not apply wads of cotton to a wound as they

will stick to the area and may cause contamination.

You should also keep some hydrogen peroxide available as it is useful in cleaning wounds and is also one of the best and simplest emetics known. Cotton applicator swabs are useful for applying ointment or removing debris from the eyes. A pair of tweezers

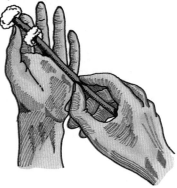

When treating an abscess, your veterinarian will begin by twisting some cotton or a cotton ball over the end of a round stick. He then will dip the cotton in an antiseptic solution and set it aside.

should also be kept handy for removing foreign bodies from the dog's throat or body.

Nearly everything a dog might contract in the way of sickness has basically the same set of symptoms: loss of appetite, diarrhea, dull eyes, dull coat, warm and/or runny nose, and a high temperature. Therefore, it is most important to take his temperature at the first sign of illness. To do this, you will need a rectal thermometer which should be lubricated

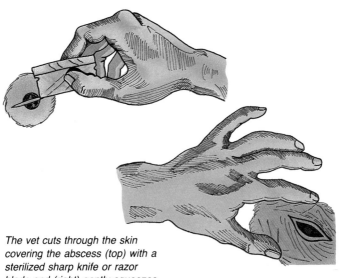

The vet cuts through the skin covering the abscess (top) with a sterilized sharp knife or razor blade and (right) gently squeezes out the pus, removing it with cotton.

with petroleum jelly. Carefully insert it into the rectum, holding it in place for at least two minutes. It must be held firmly; otherwise there is the danger of its being sucked up into the rectum, or slipping out, thus giving an inaccurate reading. The normal temperature for a dog is between 101° and 102.5°F. If your pet is seriously ill or injured in an accident, your veterinarian will advise you what to do before he arrives.

IF YOUR PET SWALLOWS POISON

A poisoned dog must be treated instantly; any delay could cause his death. Different poisons act in different ways and require different treatments. If you know the dog has swallowed an acid, alkali, gasoline, or kerosene, do not induce vomiting. Give milk to dilute the poison and rush him to the vet. If you can find the

He inserts the cotton, which is at the end of the stick, into the wound. Next he cuts off this cotton plug, as shown, and holds it in place with a piece of adhesive tape to let the wound heal from the inside out.

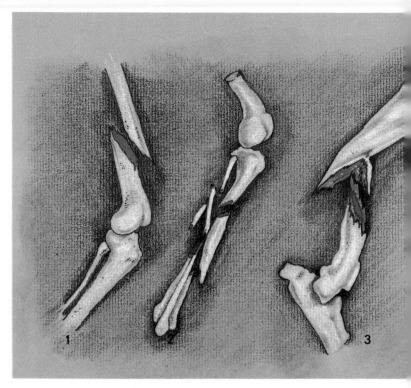

bottle or container of poison, check the label to see if there is a recommended antidote. If not, try to induce vomiting by giving him a mixture of hydrogen peroxide and water. Mix the regular drugstore strength of hydrogen peroxide (3%) with an equal part of water but do not attempt to pour it down your dog's throat as that could cause inhalation pneumonia. Instead, simply pull the dog's lips away from the side of his mouth, making a pocket for depositing the liquid. Use at least a tablespoonful of the mixture for every ten pounds of your dog's weight. He will vomit in about two minutes. When his stomach has settled, give him a teaspoonful of Epsom salts in a little water to empty the intestine quickly. The hydrogen peroxide, on ingestion, becomes oxygen and water and is harmless to your dog, but it is the best antidote for phosphorus, which is often used in rat poisons. After you have administered this emergency treatment to your pet and his stomach and bowels have been emptied, rush him to your veterinarian for further care.

DANGER IN THE HOME

There are numerous household products that can prove fatal if ingested by your pet. These include rat poison,

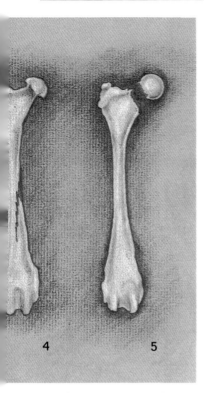

Bone fractures. 1—simple (bones don't penetrate skin); 2—comminuted (small fragments); 3—compound (bone protrudes through skin); 4—greenstick; 5—broken ball of femur.

danger lurks within the home and that is among the household plants, which are almost all poisonous, even if swallowed in small quantities. There are hundreds of poisonous plants in the United States, among which are: ivy leaves, cyclamen, lily of the valley, rhododendrons, tulip bulbs, azalea, wisteria, poinsettia leaves, mistletoe, daffodils, delphiniums, foxglove leaves, the jimson weed—we cannot name them all. Rhubarb leaves, for example, either raw or cooked, can cause death or violent convulsions. Peach, elderberry, and cherry trees can cause cyanide poisoning if their bark is consumed.

There are also many insects poisonous to dogs such as cockroaches, spiders, flies, and butterflies. Toads and frogs exude a fluid that can make a dog foam at the mouth—and even kill him—if he bites too hard!

There have been cases of dogs suffering nicotine poisoning by consuming the contents of full ashtrays which thoughtless smokers have left on the coffee table. Also, do not leave nails, staples, pins, or other sharp objects lying around and don't let your puppy play with plastic bags which could suffocate him. Unplug, remove, or cover any electrical cords or wires near your dog. Chewing live wires could lead to severe mouth burns or death. Remember that an ounce of prevention is

antifreeze, boric acid, hand soap, detergents, insecticides, mothballs, household cleansers, bleaches, de-icers, polishes and disinfectants, paints and varnish removers, acetone, turpentine, and even health and beauty aids if ingested in large enough quantities. A word to the wise should be sufficient: what you would keep locked away from your two-year-old child, also keep hidden from your pet.

There is another area where

87

worth a pound of cure: keep all potentially dangerous objects out of your pet's reach.

PROTECT YOURSELF FIRST

In almost all first aid situations, the dog is in pain. He may also be in shock and not appear to be suffering, that is until you move him. Then he may bite your hand or resist being helped at all. So if you want to help your dog, help yourself first by tying his mouth closed. To do this, use a piece of strong cloth four inches wide and three feet long, depending on the size of the dog. Make a loop in the middle of the strip and slip it over his nose with the knot under his chin and over the bony part of his nose. Pull it tight and bring the ends back around his head behind the ears and tie it tightly, ending with a bow knot for quick, easy release. Now you can handle the dog safely. As a dog perspires through his tongue, do not leave the "emergency muzzle" on any longer than necessary.

ADMINISTERING MEDICINE

When you are giving liquid medicine to your dog, it is a good idea to pull the lips away from the side of the mouth, form a lip pocket, and let the liquid trickle past the tongue. Remain at his side, never in front of the dog, as he may cough and spray you with the liquid. Moreover, you must never pour liquid medicine

directly on the tongue as inhalation pneumonia could be the disastrous result.

Medicine in pill form is best administered by forcing the dog's mouth open, holding his head back, and placing the capsule as far back on his tongue as you can reach. Put the palm of your hand over the dog's muzzle (his foreface) with your fingers on one side of his jaw, your thumb on the other. Press his lips hard against his teeth while using your other hand to pull down his lower jaw. With your two fingers, try to put the pill as far back on the dog's tongue as you can reach. Keep his mouth and nostrils closed and he should be

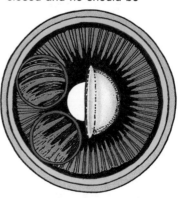

Posterior view of the eye with the lens sectioned. Eye care is important in dogs, so have your veterinarian examine your dog periodically.

forced to swallow the medicine. As the dog will not be feeling well, stroke his neck to comfort him and to help him swallow his medicine more easily. Do keep an eye on him for a few moments

If you see your dog "scooting" on its rear end or rubbing and licking its anus, the animal may have impacted anal glands. Your veterinarian will express the anal glands by first lifting the dog's tail. Next, he places his thumb and index finger on either side of the anus. He squeezes gently until the material is exuded and collects this in a paper towel or cotton gauze. The process may have to be repeated a few times.

afterward, however, to make certain that he does not spit it out.

IN CASE OF AN ACCIDENT

It is often difficult for you to assess the dog's injuries after a road accident. He may appear normal but there might be internal hemorraging. A vital organ could be damaged or ribs broken. Keep the dog as quiet and warm as possible; cover him with blankets or your coat to let his own body heat build up. Signs of shock are a rapid and weak pulse, glassy-eyed appearance, subnormal temperature, and slow capillary refill time. To determine the last symptom, press firmly against the dog's gums until they turn white. Release and count the number of seconds until the gums return to their normal color. If it is more than 2-3 seconds, the dog may be going into shock. Failure to return to the reddish pink color indicates the dog may be in serious trouble and needs immediate assistance.

If artificial respiration is required, first open the dog's mouth and check for obstructions; extend his tongue and examine the pharynx. Clear his mouth of mucus and blood and hold the mouth slightly open. Mouth-to-mouth resuscitation involves holding the dog's tongue to the bottom of his mouth with one hand and sealing his nostrils with the other while you blow into his

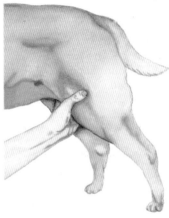

To take your dog's pulse, rest one of your fingers on the femoral artery which runs down the inner surface of his hind leg.

mouth. Watch for his chest to rise with each inflation. Repeat every 5-6 seconds or 10-12 breaths a minute.

If the veterinarian cannot come to you try to improvise a stretcher to take the dog to him. To carry a puppy, wrap him in a blanket that has been folded into several thicknesses. If he is in shock, it is better to pick him up by holding one hand under his chest, the other under the hindquarters. This will keep him stretched out.

It is always better to roll an injured dog than to try and lift him. Suppose you find him lying beside the road after a car accident. Apply a muzzle even if you have to use someone's necktie to make one. Send someone for a blanket and roll him gently onto it. Two people, one on each side, can make a stretcher out of the blanket and move the dog easily.

If no blanket is available and the injured dog must be moved, try to keep him as flat as possible. So many dogs' backs are broken in car accidents that one must first consider that possibility. However, if he can move his hind legs or tail, his spine is probably not broken. Get medical assistance for him immediately.

It should be mentioned that unfortunate car accidents, which can maim or kill your dog, can be avoided if he is confined at all times either indoors or, if out-of-doors, in a fenced-in yard or some other protective enclosure. *Never* allow your dog to roam free; even a well-trained dog may, for some unknown reason, dart into the street . . . and the result could be tragic.

If you need to walk your dog, leash him first so that he will be protected from moving vehicles.

PROTECTING YOUR PET

It is important to watch for any tell-tale signs of illness so that you can spare your pet any unnecessary suffering. Your dog's eyes, for example, should normally be bright and alert, so if the haw is bloodshot or partially covers the eye, it may be a sign of illness or irritation. If your dog has matter in the corners of his eyes, bathe them with a mild eye wash; obtain ointment or eye drops from your veterinarian to treat a chronic condition.

If your dog seems to have something wrong with his ears which causes him to scratch at them or shake his head, cautiously probe the ear with a cotton swab. An accumulation of wax will probably work itself out. Dirt or dried blood, however, is indicative of ear mites or infection and should be treated immediately. Sore ears in the summer, due to insect bites, should be washed with mild soap and water, then covered with a soothing ointment and wrapped in gauze if necessary. Keep your pet away from insects until his ears heal, even if this means confining him indoors.

INOCULATIONS

Periodic check-ups by your veterinarian throughout your puppy's life is good health insurance. The person from whom your puppy was purchased should tell you what inoculations your puppy has had and when the next visit to the vet is necessary.

An Elizabethan collar can be made by cutting a piece of heavy cardboard, as shown. Its purpose is to keep your dog from scratching a head wound or a suture.

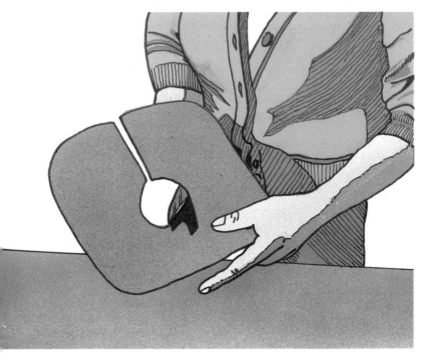

You must make certain that your puppy has been vaccinated against the following infectious canine

Unless treated promptly, the disease goes into advanced stages with infections of the lungs, intestines, and nervous

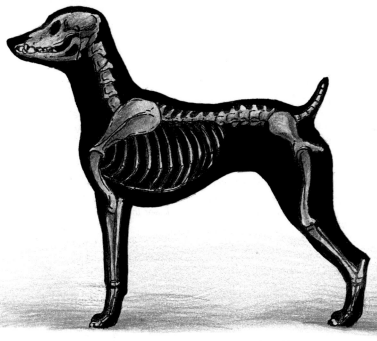

diseases: distemper, canine hepatitis, leptospirosis, rabies, parvovirus, and parainfluenza. Annual "boosters" thereafter provide inexpensive protection for your dog against such serious diseases. Puppies should also be checked for worms at an early age.

Provide your dog with a nutritional, balanced diet and opportunities for daily exercise to keep his skeletal structure healthy and strong.

DISTEMPER

Young dogs are most susceptible to distemper, although it may affect dogs of all ages. Signs of the disease are loss of appetite, depression, chills, and fever, as well as a watery discharge from the eyes and nose.

system. Dogs that recover may be impaired with paralysis, convulsions, a twitch, or some other defect, usually spastic in nature. Early inoculations in puppyhood should be followed by an annual booster to help protect against this disease.

CANINE HEPATITIS

The initial symptoms of hepatitis are drowsiness, vomiting, loss of appetite, high temperature, and great thirst. Often these symptoms are accompanied by swellings of the head, neck, and abdomen. This disease strikes quickly, and death may occur in only a few hours. An annual booster shot is needed after the initial series of puppy shots.

LEPTOSPIROSIS

Infection is begun by the dog's licking substances contaminated by the urine or feces of infected animals, and the disease is carried by bacteria that live in stagnant or slow-moving water. The symptoms are diarrhea and a yellowish-brownish discoloration of the jaws, teeth, and tongue, caused by an inflammation of the kidneys. A veterinarian can administer the leptospirosis shot along with the distemper and hepatitis shot.

RABIES

This disease of the dog's central nervous system spreads by infectious saliva which is transmitted by the bite of an infected animal. Of the two main classes of symptoms, the first is "furious rabies," in which the dog shows a period of melancholy or depression, then irritation, and finally paralysis. The first period can be from a few hours to several days, and during this time the dog is cross and will change his position often, lose his appetite, begin to lick, and bite or swallow foreign objects. During this phase the dog is spasmodically wild and has impulses to run away. The dog acts fearless and bites everything in sight. If he is caged or confined, he will fight at the bars and possibly break teeth or fracture his jaw. His bark becomes a peculiar howl. In the final stage, the animal's lower jaw becomes paralyzed and hangs down. He then walks with a stagger, and saliva drips from his mouth. About four to eight

The stifle, or knee joint, is in the dog's hind leg and is formed by the articulation of the upper and lower thighs.

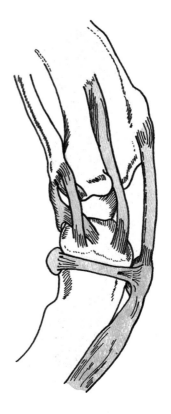

days after the onset of paralysis, the dog dies.

The second class of symptoms is referred to as "dumb rabies" and is characterized by the dog's walking in a bearlike manner with his head down. The lower jaw is paralyzed and the dog is unable to bite. It appears as if he has a bone caught in his throat.

health department must be notified in the case of a rabid dog, for this is a danger to all who come near him. As with the other shots each year, an annual rabies inoculation is very important. In many areas, the administration of rabies vaccines for dogs is required by law.

Dorsal view of the canine heart.

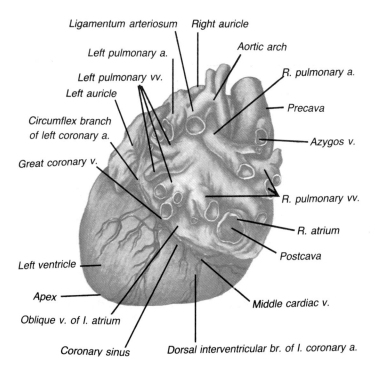

Ligamentum arteriosum
Right auricle
Left pulmonary a.
Aortic arch
Left pulmonary vv.
R. pulmonary a.
Left auricle
Circumflex branch of left coronary a.
Precava
Great coronary v.
Azygos v.
R. pulmonary vv.
R. atrium
Left ventricle
Postcava
Apex
Oblique v. of l. atrium
Middle cardiac v.
Coronary sinus
Dorsal interventricular br. of l. coronary a.

If a dog is bitten by a rabid animal, he probably can be saved if he is taken to a veterinarian in time for a series of injections. After the symptoms appear, however, no cure is possible. The local

PARVOVIRUS

This relatively new virus is a contagious disease that has spread in almost epidemic proportions throughout certain sections of the United States. Also, it has appeared

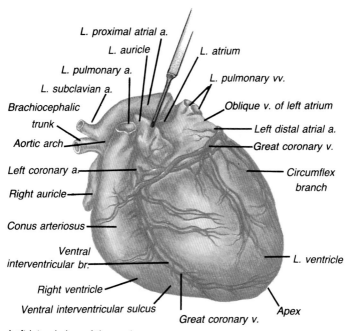

L. proximal atrial a.

L. auricle

L. atrium

L. pulmonary a.

L. pulmonary vv.

L. subclavian a.

Brachiocephalic trunk

Oblique v. of left atrium

Left distal atrial a.

Aortic arch

Great coronary v.

Left coronary a.

Circumflex branch

Right auricle

Conus arteriosus

Ventral interventricular br.

L. ventricle

Right ventricle

Ventral interventricular sulcus

Great coronary v.

Apex

Left lateral view of the canine heart.

in Australia, Canada, and Europe. Canine parvovirus attacks the intestinal tract, white blood cells, and heart muscle. It is believed to spread through dog-to-dog contact, and the specific course of infection seems to come from fecal matter of infected dogs. Overcoming parvovirus is difficult, for it is capable of existing in the environment for many months under varying conditions and temperatures, and it can be transmitted from place to place on the hair and feet of infected dogs, as well as on the clothes and shoes of people.

Vomiting and severe diarrhea, which will appear within five to seven days after the animal has been exposed to the virus, are the initial signs of this disease. At the onset of illness, feces will be light gray or yellow-gray in color, and the urine might be blood-streaked. Because of the vomiting and severe diarrhea, the dog that has contracted the disease will dehydrate quickly. Depression and loss of appetite, as well as a rise in temperature, can accompany the other symptoms. Death caused by this disease usually occurs within 48 to 72 hours following the appearance of the symptoms. Puppies are hardest hit, and the virus is fatal to 75 percent of puppies that contract it. Death in puppies can be within two days of the onset of the illness.

A series of shots administered by a veterinarian is the best preventive measure for canine parvovirus. It is also important to disinfect the area where the dog is housed by using

Your local pet shop can advise you on which type of shampoo best suits the needs of your dog. If he is plagued with fleas or ticks, there are special preparations available.

one part sodium hypochlorite solution (household bleach) to thirty parts of water and to keep the dog from coming into contact with the fecal matter of other dogs.

PARAINFLUENZA

Parainfluenza, or infectious canine tracheobronchitis, is commonly known as "kennel cough." It is highly contagious, affects the upper respiratory system, and is spread through direct or indirect contact with already diseased dogs. It will readily infect dogs of all ages that have not been vaccinated or that were previously infected. While this condition is definitely one of the serious diseases in dogs, it is self-limiting, usually lasting only two to four weeks. The symptoms are high fever and intense, harsh coughing that brings up mucus. As long as your pet sees your veterinarian immediately, the chances for his complete recovery are excellent.

EXTERNAL PARASITES

A parasite is an animal that lives in or on an organism of another species known as the host. The majority of dogs' skin problems are parasitic in nature and an estimated 90% of puppies are born with parasites.

Ticks can cause serious problems to dogs where the

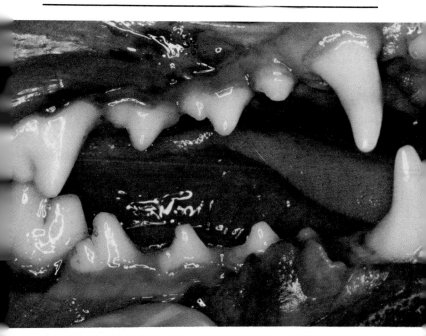

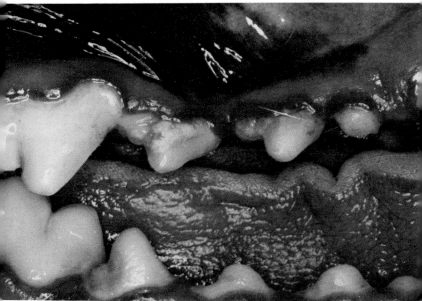

In the top photo, the gums appear healthy and the tooth surfaces are relatively clean, while in the lower photo, the gums are moderately to severely inflamed and a great deal of plaque and calculus are present. These photos serve to illustrate the importance of canine dental care. Photos courtesy of Dr. J. Hock, School of Dental Medicine, University of Connecticut.

latter have access to woods, fields, and vegetation in which large numbers of native mammals live. Ticks are usually found clinging to vegetation and attach themselves to animals passing by. They have eight legs and a heavy shield or shell-like covering on their upper surface. Only by keeping dogs away from tick-infested areas can ticks on dogs be prevented.

The flea is the single most common cause of skin and coat problems in dogs. There are 11,000 kinds of fleas

The common dog flea, magnified a great number of times. If your dog has fleas, not only will you have to treat him, but you will have to treat his entire environment as well; in other words, you will have to attack on two fronts.

A greatly magnified drawing of a tick. Check your dog's coat often for these pesky parasites, particularly during the warm-weather months.

which can transmit specific disorders like tapeworm and heartworm or transport smaller parasites onto your dog. The common tapeworm, for example, requires the flea as an intermediate host for completion of its life cycle. A female flea can lay hundreds of eggs and these will become adults in less than three weeks. Depending on the temperature and the amount

of moisture, large numbers of fleas can attack dogs, and the ears of dogs, in particular, can play host to hundreds of fleas.

Fleas can lurk in crevices and cracks, carpets, and bedding for months, so frequent cleaning of your dog's environment is absolutely essential. If he is infected by other dogs, then have him bathed and "dipped," which means that he will be put into water containing a chemical that kills fleas. Your veterinarian will advise which dip to use and your dog must be bathed.

These parasites are tenacious and remarkably agile creatures; fleas have existed since prehistoric times and have been found in arctic as well as tropical climates. Some experts claim that fleas can jump 150 times the length of their bodies; this makes them difficult to catch and kill.

Thus, treating your pet for parasites without simultaneously treating the environment is both inefficient and ineffective.

INTERNAL PARASITES

Four common internal parasites that may infect a dog are: roundworms, hookworms, whipworms, and tapeworms. The first three can be diagnosed by laboratory examination of the dog's stool, and tapeworms can be determined by seeing segments in the stool or attached to the hair around the anus. When a veterinarian determines what type of worm or worms are present, he then can advise the best treatment.

Roundworms, the dog's most common intestinal parasite, have a life cycle which permits complete eradication by worming twice, ten days apart. The first worming will remove all adults and the second will destroy all subsequently hatched eggs

This is the mite that causes red mange. Here it is enlarged, but in reality it is microscopic.

The sarcoptic mange mite burrows into the dog's skin where it creates havoc. Sarcoptic mange is contagious, and young pups are especially susceptible.

before they, in turn, can produce more parasites.

A dog in good physical condition is less susceptible to worm infestation than a weak dog. Proper sanitation and a nutritious diet help in preventing worms. One of the best preventive measures is to have clean, dry bedding for the dog, as this diminishes the possibility of reinfection due to flea or tick bites.

99

Heartworm infestation in dogs is passed by mosquitoes. Dogs with this disease tire easily, have difficulty in breathing, and lose weight despite a hearty appetite. Administration of preventive medicine throughout the spring, summer, and fall months is advised. A veterinarian must first take a blood sample from the dog to test for the presence of the disease, and if the dog is heartworm-free, pills or liquid medicine can be prescribed to protect against any infestation.

CANINE SENIOR CITIZENS

The processes of aging and gradual degenerative changes start far earlier in a dog than often observed, usually at about seven years of age. If we recall that each year of a dog's life roughly corresponds to about seven years in the life of a man, by the age of seven he is well into middle age. Your pet will become less active, will have a poorer appetite with increased thirst, there will be frequent periods of constipation and less than normal passage of urine. His skin and coat might become dull and dry and his hair will become thin and fall out. There is a tendency towards obesity in old age, which should be avoided by maintaining a regular exercise program. Remember, also, that your pet will be less able to cope with extreme heat,

cold, fatigue, and change in routine.

There is the possibility of loss or impairment of hearing or eyesight. He may become bad-tempered more often

than in the past. Other ailments such as rheumatism, arthritis, kidney infections, heart disease, male prostatism, and hip dysplasia may occur. Of course, all these require a veterinarian's examination and recommendation of suitable treatment. Care of the teeth is also important in the aging dog. Indeed, the mouth can be a barometer of nutritional health. Degenerating gums, heavy tartar on the teeth, loose teeth, and sore lips are common. The worst of all diseases in old age, however, is neglect. Good care in early life will have its effect on your dog's later years; the nutrition and general health care of his first few years can determine his lifespan and the quality of his life. It is worth bearing in mind that the older, compared to the younger, animal needs more protein of good biological value, more vitamins A, B-complex, D and

DEATH OF A FRIEND

What can you do, however, for a pet who is so sick or severely injured that he will never recover his normal health? Although one is often

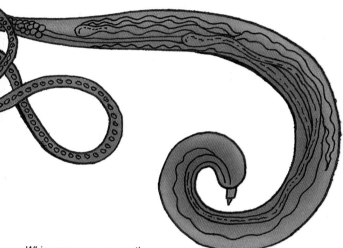

Whipworms are among the many internal parasites that can attack dogs. Your veterinarian is best qualified to detect the presence of worms, if they exist, in your dog.

E, more calcium and iron, less fat and fewer carbohydrates.

The companionship of pets, not only to children and adults, but particularly to the aged and lonely, cannot be overestimated. Therefore, a dog's grateful owner should do all he can to enhance and prolong the life of his cherished companion. Regular doses of TLC or Tender Loving Care is the best "medicine" your dog can receive throughout his life.

extremely reluctant to consider the suggestion, sometimes the kindest and most humane solution is to have your veterinarian put him out of his misery by inducing his death peacefully and painlessly. This process is called euthanasia, a word of Greek derivation meaning "easy or good death." It is usually carried out by having your veterinarian inject a death-inducing drug or an overdose of anesthetic.

Such a decision will probably be an extremely difficult one for you to make but you need not, in fact, should not, make it alone.

Your veterinarian should be your chief adviser and family and friends can assist in the decision-making process. Your children should not be excluded from this painful time; it would be inadvisable to attempt to "shield" or "protect" them from such events which are an inevitable part of life. They would suffer even more if, later, they did not understand how or why their beloved pet had died.

memories. People who do not have pets often fail to realize what a very important part of our lives these animals fill and what a void is created by their absence. Others are more sympathetic and compassionate. Rest assured,

Digestive action usually slows down as your dog ages, so check with your veterinarian about your canine senior citizen's special dietary needs.

CANINE DIGESTIVE APPARATUS

Bile duct
Pancreatic duct
Accessory pancreatic duct
Pancreas—right lobe (covering right kidney)
Ascending colon
Cecum
Duodenum
Stomach
Pancreas—left lobe
Transverse colon
Descending colon
Spleen
Left kidney

By remembering the wonderful times with your pet, by talking about him to family and friends, by remembering him as healthy and full of life, you will eventually cope with your grief. It is perfectly natural to grieve for the loss of such a loyal, affectionate companion who has provided you with so many happy

however, that if you have chosen a painless, eternal sleep for your pet by "putting him to sleep" (an appropriate euphemism in this case), you have done him a final service as a loving, considerate friend.

Breeding

If you own a bitch and you want to breed her, first make sure you can handle the responsibility of caring for her and her litter of pups. Consider the time and money involved just to get her into breeding condition and then to sustain her throughout pregnancy and afterwards while she tends her young. You will be obligated to house, feed, groom, and housebreak the puppies until good homes can be found for them; and, lest we forget, there will be periodic trips to the vet for check-ups, wormings, and inoculations. Common sense should tell you that it is indeed cruel to bring unwanted or unplanned puppies into an already crowded canine world; only negligent pet owners allow this to happen. With pet-quality purebred dogs, most breeders require prospective pet owners to sign a neuter/spay agreement when they purchase their dogs. In this way breeders can be assured that only their very best stock of show-quality and breeder-quality animals, *i.e.,* those that match closely their individual standards of perfection and those that are free of genetic disorders or disease, will be used to propagate the breed.

Before you select a stud to mate with your bitch, think carefully about why you want her to give birth to a litter of puppies. If you feel she will be deprived in some way if she is

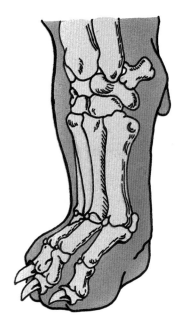

Anatomy of the dog's foot. Infections between the toes are quite common in the older dog, as he tends to have a lowered resistance to disease, less vitality, and a less active circulation. This is why it is important to check your aging dog's feet regularly.

not bred, if you think your children will learn from the experience, if you have the mistaken notion that you will make money from this great undertaking, think again. A dog can lead a perfectly happy, healthy, normal life without having been mated; in fact, spaying a female and neutering a male help them become better pets, as they are not so anxious to search for a mate in an effort to relieve their sexual tensions. As for giving the children a lesson in sex education, this is hardly a valid reason for breeding your dog. And on an economic level, it takes not only years of hard work (researching pedigrees and bloodlines, studying genetics, among other things), but it takes plenty of capital (money, equipment, facilities) to make a decent profit from dog breeding. Why most dedicated breeders are lucky just to break even. If you have

THE FEMALE "IN SEASON"

A bitch may come into season (also known as "heat" or estrus) once or several times a year, depending on the particular breed and the individual dog. Her first seasonal period, that is to say, the time when she is capable of being fertilized by a male dog, may occur as early as six months with some breeds. If you own a female and your intention is *not* to

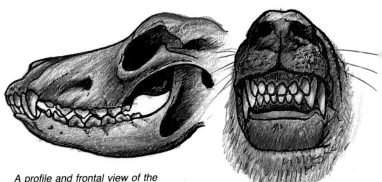

A profile and frontal view of the scissors bite, in which the lower teeth touch the inside of the upper teeth.

only a casual interest in dog breeding, it is best to leave this pastime to those who are more experienced in such matters, those who consider it a serious hobby or vocation. If you have bought a breeder– or show-quality canine, one that may be capable of producing champions, and if you are just starting out with this breeding venture, seek advice from the seller of your dog, from other veteran breeders, and from your veterinarian before you begin.

breed her, by all means discuss with the vet the possibility of having her spayed: this means before she reaches sexual maturity.

The first sign of the female's being in season is a thin red discharge, which may increase for about a week; it then changes color to a thin yellowish stain, which lasts about another week. Simultaneously, there is a swelling of the vulva, the exterior portion of the female's reproductive tract; the soft, flabby vulva indicates her readiness to mate.

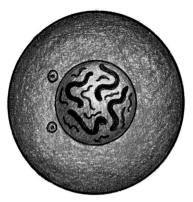

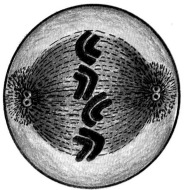

Mitosis, or cell division, beginning. The chromosomes (top left) are becoming thicker and more obvious in the cell's nucleus. The spindle, a web of fibers, forms (top right) and covers the middle of the cell. The nucleus disappears and the chromosomes split and are pulled to opposite sides of the cell. (Below) the cell has almost divided into two.

Around this second week or so ovulation occurs, and this is the crucial period for her to be bred, if this is what you have in mind for her. It is during this middle phase of the heat cycle when conception can take place. Just remember that there is great variation from bitch to bitch with regard to how often they come into heat, how long the heat cycles last, how long the period of ovulation lasts, and how much time elapses between heat cycles. Generally, after the third week of heat, the vulval swelling decreases and the estrus period ceases for several months.

It should be mentioned that the female will probably lose her puppy coat, or at least shed part of it, about three months after she has come into season. This is the time when her puppies would have been weaned, had she been mated, and females generally

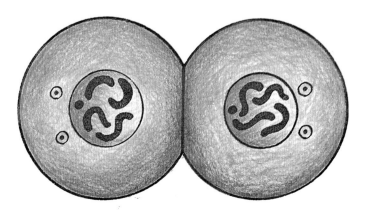

drop coat at this time.

With female dogs, there are few, if any, behavioral changes during estrus. A bitch may dart out of an open door to greet all available male dogs that show an interest in her, and she may occasionally raise her tail and assume a mating stance, particularly if you pet her lower back; but these signs are not as dramatic as those of the sexually mature male. He himself does not experience heat cycles;

Three types of bites seen in dogs: top, scissors; middle, overshot; and bottom, undershot.

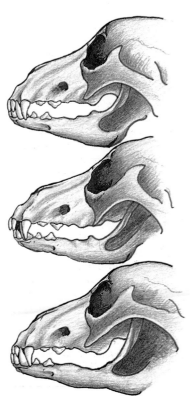

rather, he is attracted to the female during all phases of her seasonal period. He usually becomes more aggressive and tends to fight with other males, especially over females in heat. He tends to mark his territory with urine to attract females and at the same time to warn other competitive males. It is not uncommon to see him mount various objects, and people, in an effort to satisfy his mature sexual urges.

If you are a homeowner and you have an absolutely climb-proof and dig-proof run within your yard, it may be safe to leave your bitch in season there. But then again it may not be a wise idea, as there have been cases of males mating with females right through chain-link fencing! Just to be on the safe side, shut her indoors during her heat periods and don't let her outdoors until you are certain the estrus period is over. Never leave a bitch in heat outdoors, unsupervised, even for a minute so that she can defecate or urinate. If you want to prevent the neighborhood dogs from hanging around your doorstep, as they inevitably will do when they discover your female is in season, take her some distance away from the house before you let her do her business. Otherwise, these canine suitors will be attracted to her by the arousing odor of her urine, and they will know instinctively that she isn't far from her scented "calling card." If you need to walk your bitch, take her in the car to a nearby park or field for a chance to stretch her legs. Remember that after about three weeks, and this varies from dog to dog, you can let her outdoors again with no

(vacations, business trips, social engagements, and so on). Make sure you will be able to set aside plenty of

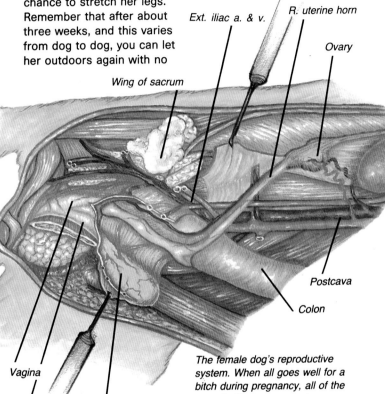

Ext. iliac a. & v.

R. uterine horn

Ovary

Wing of sacrum

Postcava

Colon

Vagina

Bladder

Urethra

The female dog's reproductive system. When all goes well for a bitch during pregnancy, all of the reproductive organs work together in harmony.
(a. = artery; v. = vein; r. = right; Ext. = external).

worry that she can have puppies until the next heat period.

WHEN TO BREED

It is usually best to breed a bitch when she comes into her second or third season. Plan in advance the time of year which is best for you, taking into account your own schedule of activities

time to assist with whelping of the newborn pups and caring for the dam and her litter for the next few weeks. At the very least, it probably will take an hour or so each day just to feed and clean up after the brood—but undoubtedly you will find it takes much longer if you stop to admire and play with the youngsters periodically! Refrain from selling the litter until it is at least six weeks old, keeping in mind that a litter of pups takes up a fair amount of

Hopefully, as strongly recommended, you will have already lined up buyers for the pups in advance of their arrival into this world.

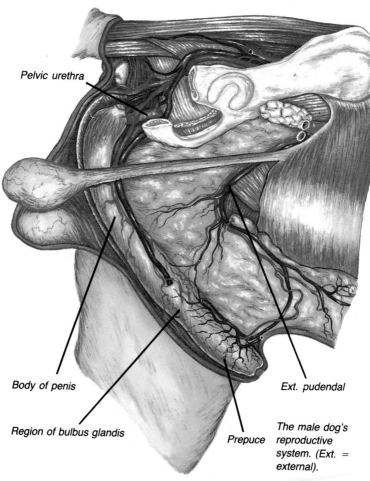

Pelvic urethra

Body of penis

Region of bulbus glandis

Ext. pudendal

Prepuce

The male dog's reproductive system. (Ext. = external).

space by then. It will be your responsibility to provide for them until they have been weaned from their mother, properly socialized, housebroken, and ready to go to new homes (unless you plan to keep them all).

CHOOSING THE STUD

You can plan to breed your female about six-and-one-half months after the start of her last season, although a variation of a month or two either way is not unusual. Do some research into the various bloodlines within your breed and then choose a stud dog and make arrangements well in advance. If you are breeding for show stock, which will command higher prices than pet-quality animals, a mate should be chosen very carefully. He should complement any deficiencies (bad traits) that your female may have, and he should have a good show record or be the sire of show winners, if he is old enough to have proven himself. If possible, the bitch and stud should have several ancestors in common within the last two or three generations, as such combinations have been known, generally, to "click" best.

The owner of a stud dog usually charges a stud fee for use of the animal's services. This does not always guarantee a litter, but if she fails to conceive, chances are

you may be able to breed your female to that stud again. In some instances the owner of the stud will agree to take a "first pick of the litter" in place of a fee. You should, of course, settle all details beforehand, including the possibility of a single puppy surviving, deciding the age at which the pup is to be taken, and so forth.

If you plan to raise a litter that will be sold exclusively as pets, and if you merely plan to make use of an available male (not a top stud dog), the most important selection point involves temperament. Make sure the dog is friendly, as well as healthy, because a bad disposition can be passed on to his puppies—and this is the worst of all traits in a dog destined to be a pet. If you are breeding pet-quality dogs, a "stud fee puppy," not necessarily the choice of the litter, is the usual payment. Don't breed indiscriminately; be sure you will be able to find good homes for each of the pups, or be sure you have the

Although full dentition is most desirable in show dogs, it is not uncommon to find dogs with missing teeth.

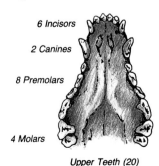

6 Incisors

2 Canines

8 Premolars

4 Molars

Upper Teeth (20)

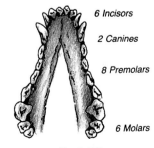

6 Incisors

2 Canines

8 Premolars

6 Molars

Lower Teeth (22)

Correct Dentition

facilities to keep them yourself, *before* you plan to mate your dog.

PREPARATION FOR BREEDING

Before you breed your female, make sure she is in good health. She should be neither too thin nor too fat. Any skin disease *must* be cured first so that it is not passed on to the puppies. If she has worms, she should be wormed before being bred or within three weeks after the mating. It is generally considered a good idea to revaccinate her against distemper and hepatitis before the puppies are born. This will increase the immunity the puppies receive during their early, most vulnerable period.

The female will probably be ready to breed twelve days after the first colored discharge appears. You can usually make arrangements to board her with the owner of the stud for a few days, to insure her being there at the proper time; or you can take her to be mated and bring her home the same day if you live near enough to the stud's owner. If the bitch still appears receptive she may be bred again two days later, just to make certain the mating was successful. However, some females never show signs of willingness, so it helps to have an experienced breeder on hand. In fact, you both may have to assist with

Facing page: lifecycle of a dog tapeworm. Fleas swallow tapeworm eggs which develop into larvae inside them. When a dog eats an infected flea, the larvae transform into the head (or scolex) of the adult tapeworm. The scolex attaches to the dog's intestinal lining and develops egg-containing segments that are passed out with the dog's feces, and the cycle continues.

the mating by holding the animals against each other to ensure the "tie" is not broken, that is, to make certain copulation takes place. Sometimes, too, you'll need to muzzle the bitch to keep her from biting you or the stud.

Usually the second day after the discharge changes color is the proper time to mate the bitch, and she may be bred for about three days following this time. For an additional week or so, she may have some discharge and attract other dogs by her odor; but she should not be bred. Once she has been bred, keep her far from all other male dogs, as they have the capacity to impregnate her again and sire some of her puppies. This could prove disastrous where purebred puppies—especially show-quality ones—are concerned.

THE FEMALE IN WHELP

You can expect the puppies nine weeks from the day of the mating, although sixty-one days is as common as sixty-three. Gestation, that period

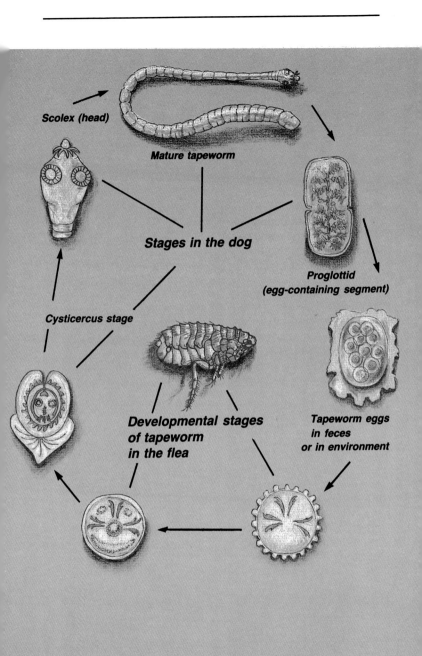

Scolex (head)

Mature tapeworm

Stages in the dog

Proglottid
(egg-containing segment)

Cysticercus stage

Developmental stages
of tapeworm
in the flea

Tapeworm eggs
in feces
or in environment

when the pups are developing inside their mother, varies among individual bitches. During this time the female should receive normal care and exercise. If she was overweight at the start, don't increase her food right away; excess weight at whelping time can be a problem with some dogs. If she is on the thin side, however, supplement her meal or meals with a portion of milk and biscuit at noontime. This will help build her up and put weight on her.

You may want to add a mineral and vitamin supplement to her diet, on the advice of your veterinarian, since she will need an extra supply not only for herself but for the puppies growing inside

mother will have little room for food and less of an appetite. She should be tempted with meat, liver, and milk, however.

As the female in whelp grows heavier, cut out violent exercise and jumping from her usual routine. Although a dog used to such activities will often play with the children or run around voluntarily, restrain her for her own sake.

A sign that whelping is imminent is the loss of hair around her breasts. This is nature's way of "clearing a path" so that the puppies will be able to find their source of nourishment. As parturition

Vitamins and minerals are a vital part of the pregnant bitch's diet.

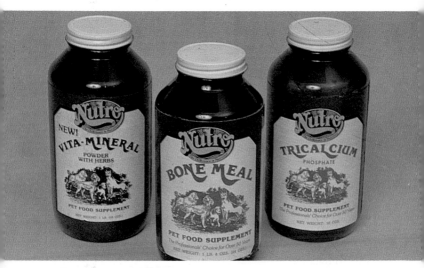

of her. As the mother's appetite increases, feed her more. During the last two weeks of pregnancy, the pups grow enormously and the

draws near, the breasts will have swelled with milk and the nipples will have enlarged and darkened to a rosy pink. If the hair in the breast region does

Fertilization is the union of two special cells, the egg from the female and the sperm from the male. One of these sperm has penetrated the membrane that surrounds the egg.

such as a corner of your cellar or garage (provided these places are warm and dry). An unused room, such as a dimly

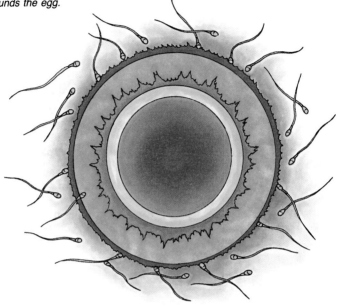

not shed for some reason, you can easily cut it short with a pair of scissors or comb it out so that it does not mat and become a hindrance to the suckling pups later on.

PREPARING FOR THE PUPPIES

Prepare a whelping box a few days before the puppies are due, and allow the mother to sleep there overnight or to spend some time in it during the day to become accustomed to it. Then she is less likely to try to have her pups under the front porch or in the middle of your bed. A variety of places will serve,

lit spare bedroom, can also serve as the place for delivery. If the weather is warm, a large outdoor dog house will do, as long as it is well protected from rain, drafts, and the cold—and enclosed by fencing or a run. A whelping box serves to separate mother and puppies from visitors and other distractions. The walls should be high enough to restrain the puppies yet low enough to allow the mother to take a short respite from her brood after she has fed them. Four feet square is minimum size (for most dogs) and six-to-eight-inch high walls will keep

113

the pups in until they begin to climb; then side walls should be built up so that the young ones cannot wander away from their nest. As the puppies grow, they really need more room anyway, so double the space with a very low partition down the middle of the box, and soon you will find them naturally housebreaking themselves. Puppies rarely relieve themselves where they sleep.

Layers of newspapers spread over the whole area will make excellent bedding and be absorbent enough to keep the surface warm and dry. These should be removed daily and replaced with another thick layer. An old quilt or washable blanket makes better footing for the nursing puppies than slippery newspaper during the first week; this is also softer for the mother to lie on.

Be prepared for the actual whelping several days in advance. Usually the mother will tear up papers, refuse food, and become restless. These may be false alarms; the real test is her temperature, which will drop to below 100°F about twelve hours before whelping. Take her temperature with a rectal thermometer, morning and evening, and usher her to her whelping box when her temperature goes down. Keep a close watch on her and make sure she stays safely indoors (or outdoors in a safe enclosure); if she is let

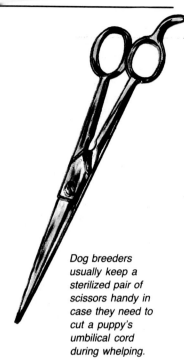

Dog breeders usually keep a sterilized pair of scissors handy in case they need to cut a puppy's umbilical cord during whelping.

outside, unleashed, or allowed to roam freely, she could wander off and start to go into labor. It is possible that she could whelp anywhere and this could be unfortunate if she needs your assistance.

WHELPING

Usually little help is needed from you, but it is wise to stay close to make sure that the mother's lack of experience (if this is her first time) does not cause an unnecessary complication. Be ready to help when the first puppy arrives, for it could smother if she does not break the amniotic membrane enclosing it. She should tear open the sac and start licking the puppy, drying and stimulating it. Check to see that all fluids have been cleared from the pup's nostrils and mouth after the mother has licked her youngster clean; otherwise, the pup may have difficulty breathing. If the mother fails to tear open the sac and stimulate the newborn's breathing, you can do this yourself by tearing the sac with your hands and then gently rubbing the infant with a soft, rough towel. The afterbirth, attached to the puppy by the long umbilical cord, should follow the birth of each puppy. Watch to make sure that each afterbirth is expelled, for the retaining of this material can cause infection. In her instinct for

stimulate her milk supply, as well as labor, for remaining pups. But eating too many afterbirths can make her lose appetite for the food she needs to feed her pups and regain her strength. So remove the rest of them, along with the wet newspapers, and keep the box dry and clean.

If the mother does not bite the cord, or bites it too close to the puppy's body, take over the job to prevent an umbilical hernia. Tearing is recommended; but you can

Whelping boxes can be constructed of smooth wood. Make sure you include a "pig rail" around the inside perimeter of the box to keep the mother from crushing her pups.

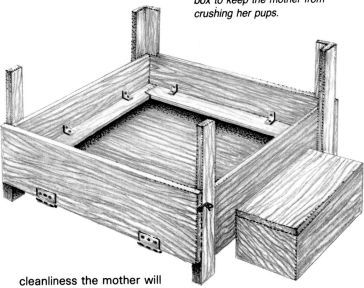

cleanliness the mother will probably eat the afterbirth after severing the umbilical cord. One or two meals of this will not hurt her; they

cut the cord, about two inches from the body, with a sawing motion of scissors

that have been sterilized in alcohol. Then dip the end of the cut cord in a shallow dish of iodine; the cord will dry up and fall off in a few days.

The puppies may follow each other in a few minutes or a few hours, as the time varies with each bitch. If she is actively straining without producing a puppy, the youngster may be presented backward, a so-called "breech" birth. Careful assistance with a well-lubricated finger to feel for the puppy or ease it back may help, but never attempt to pull it out by force. This could cause serious damage, so seek the services of an expert—your veterinarian or an experienced breeder.

If *anything* seems wrong, during labor or parturition, waste no time in calling your veterinarian who can examine the bitch and, if necessary, give her hormones to stimulate the birth of the remaining puppies. You may want his experience in whelping the litter even if all goes well. He will probably prefer to have the puppies

The shoulder and arm musculature. Unless your dog has suffered a serious injury or was born with a congenital defect, his bones, muscles, and joints should remain healthy until he reaches middle age— around five or six years old.

born at his hospital rather than to get up in the middle of the night to come to your home. The mother would, no doubt, prefer to stay at home; but you can be sure she will get the best of care in a veterinary hospital. If the puppies are born at home and all goes as it should, watch the mother carefully afterward. Within a day or two of the birth, it is wise to have the veterinarian check her and the pups to ensure all is well.

Make sure each puppy finds a teat and starts nursing right away, as these first few meals supply colostral antibodies to help the pup fight disease. As soon as he is dry, hold each puppy to a nipple for a good meal without competition. Then he may join his littermates in the whelping box, out of his mother's way while she continues giving birth. Keep a supply of evaporated milk on hand for emergency feedings or later weaning. A formula of evaporated milk, corn syrup, and a little water with egg yolk should be warmed and fed in a doll's or baby's bottle if necessary. Or purchase a pet nurser kit to have on hand; these are available in local pet shops. A supplementary feeding often helps weak pups (those that may have difficulty nursing) over the hump. Keep track of birth weights and weekly readings thereafter; this will furnish an accurate record of the pups' growth and health, and the information will be valuable for your veterinarian.

RAISING THE PUPPIES

After the puppies have been born, take the mother outside for a walk and drink of water, and then leave her to take care of her brood. She will probably not want to stay away more than a minute or two for the first few weeks. Be sure to keep water available at all times and feed her milk or broth frequently, as she needs liquids to produce milk. Encourage her to eat, with her favorite foods, until she seeks it of her own accord. She will soon develop a ravenous appetite and should have at least two large meals a day, with dry food available in addition. Your veterinarian can guide you on the finer points of nutrition as they apply to nursing dams.

Prepare a warm place to put the puppies after they are born to keep them dry and help them to a good start in life. An electric heating pad or hot water bottle covered with flannel can be placed in the bottom of a cardboard box and near the mother so that she can see her puppies. She will usually allow you to help her care for the youngsters, but don't take them out of her

sight. Let her handle things if your interference seems to make her nervous.

Be sure that all the puppies are getting enough to eat. If

Normally the dam will cut the umbilical cord with her teeth. The short stub that remains dries up and falls off in a couple of days.

the mother sits or stands instead of lying still to nurse, the probable cause is scratching from the puppies' nails. You can remedy this by clipping them, as you would the bitch's, with a pet nail clipper. Or manicure scissors will do for these tiny claws. Some breeders advise disposing of the smaller or weaker pups in a large litter, as the mother has trouble handling more than six or seven. You can help her out by preparing an extra puppy box or basket furnished with a heating pad and some bedding material. Leave half the litter with the mother and the other half in the extra box, changing off at two-hour intervals at first. Later you may exchange them less frequently, leaving them all together except during the day. Try supplementary feedings, too; as soon as their eyes open, at about two weeks, they will lap from a small dish.

WEANING THE PUPPIES

Normally the puppies should be completely weaned at five weeks, although you can start to feed them at three weeks. They will find it easier to lap semi-solid food than to drink milk at first, so mix baby cereal with whole or evaporated milk, warmed to body temperature, and offer it to the puppies in a saucer. Until they learn to lap it, it is best to feed one or two at a time because they are more likely to walk into it than to eat it. Hold the saucer at their

Pet shops stock pet nurser kits for those dog owners who need to hand-feed their puppies. Such kits come complete with bottle, nipples, and bottle brush.

chin level, and let them gather around, keeping paws out of the dish. A damp sponge afterward prevents most of the cereal from sticking to the skin if the mother doesn't clean them up. Once they have gotten the idea, broth or babies' meat soup may be alternated with milk, and you can start them on finely chopped meat. At about four weeks, they will eat four meals a day and soon do without their mother entirely. Start them on canned dog food, or leave dry puppy food with them in a dish for self-feeding. Don't leave water with them all the time; at this age everything is a play toy and they will use it as a wading pool. They can drink all they need if it is offered several times a day, after

meals. As the puppies grow up the mother will go into their "pen" only to nurse them, first sitting up and then standing. To dry up her milk

The puppies may be put outside during the day, unless it is too cold or rainy, as soon as their eyes are open. They will benefit from the sunlight.

supply completely, keep the mother away for longer periods; after a few days of part-time nursing she can stay away for even longer periods, and then permanently. The little milk left will be resorbed by her body.

Chocolate Nylabones® and similar products are ideal for puppies. They have a very thin layer of chocolate deposited UNDER the surface of the bone. The flavor is released as the dog chews on the knuckle. The bone must be replaced when the knuckle is worn down.

A rubber mat or newspapers underneath will protect them from cold or dampness. As they mature, the pups can be let out for longer intervals, although make sure you provide them with a shelter at night or in bad weather. By now, cleaning up after the matured youngsters is a man-sized job, so put them out at least during the day and make your task easier. If you enclose them in a run or kennel, remember to clean it *daily,* as various parasites and other infectious organisms may be lurking if the quarters are kept dirty.

present. If one puppy is infected then all should be wormed as a preventive measure. Follow the veterinarian's advice; this also applies to vaccinations. If you plan to keep a pup yourself, you will want to vaccinate him, and his littermates, at the earliest age. This way, those pups destined for new homes will be protected against some of the more debilitating canine diseases.

THE DECISION TO SPAY OR NEUTER

If you decide not to use your male or female for

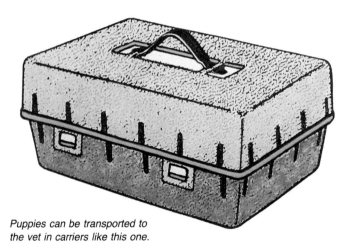

Puppies can be transported to the vet in carriers like this one.

You can expect the pups to need at least one worming before they are ready to go to new homes; so for each animal, before they are three weeks old, take a stool sample to your veterinarian. The vet can determine, by analyzing the stool, if any of the pups have worms—and if so, what kind of worms are

breeding, or if you are obligated to have the animal altered based on an agreement made between you and the seller, make the necessary arrangements with your veterinarian as soon as possible. The surgery involved for both males and females is relatively simple and painless: males will be castrated and

females will have their ovaries and uterus removed. In both cases, the operation does not alter their personalities; you will, however, notice that males will be less likely to roam, to get into fights with other male dogs, and to mount objects and people. From a pet owner's point of view, an animal that is less anxious and less inclined to wander off in search of a mate makes a better companion.

Your veterinarian can best determine at what age neutering or spaying should be done. With a young female dog, the operation may be somewhat more involved, and as a result be more costly; however, in the long run you will be glad you made the decision to have this done for your pet. After a night or two at the veterinarian's or an animal hospital, your bitch can be safely returned to your home. Her stitches will heal in a short time, and when they are removed, you will hardly notice her souvenir scar of the routine operation. Once she has been spayed, she no longer will be capable of having a litter of puppies.

Check with your city or town or with the local humane society for special programs that are available for pet owners. In many municipalities you can have your pet altered for just a

Tomarctus was an early ancestor of the family Canidae, which includes not only dogs, but wolves, coyotes, jackals, foxes, and other mammals.

small fee; the low price is meant to encourage pet owners to take advantage of this important means of birth control for their dogs. Pet adoption agencies and other animal welfare organizations can house only so many animals at one time, given the money, space, and other resources they have available. This is why pet owners are urged to have their pets altered, so that puppies, resulting from accidental breedings, won't end up being put to sleep as so many others have that are lost, stray, unwanted, or abandoned.

Suggested Reading

The following books, available at most pet shops and book stores, are recommended for your reading pleasure.

HOW TO SHOW YOUR OWN DOG
By Virginia Tuck Nichols
ISBN 0-87666-661-6
PS-607

You don't necessarily need a professional handler to show your dog. What you do need is some basic information about dog shows, how a champion is made, what the terms and definitions are, and how to prepare for the big day.
Hard cover, 5½" x 8½", 288 pages 136 black and white photos; 10 line illustrations

DOG BEHAVIOR
By Dr. Ian Dunbar
ISBN 0-87666-671-3
H-1016

A book intended for everyone who likes dogs and wants to understand them better as well as for anyone interested in animal behavior.
Hard cover, 5½" x 8", 223 pages 20 full-color photos, 115 black and white photos, 3 line drawings

ENCYCLOPEDIA OF DOG BREEDS
By Ernest H. Hart
ISBN 0-87666-285-8
H-927

This comprehensive volume includes everything you need to know about feeding, basic dog training, dog diseases and first aid, and showing. All of the various dog groups are covered in depth.
Hard cover, 5½" x 8½", 784 pages 537 black and white photos; 138 color photos

DOG TRAINING
By Lew Burke
ISBN 0-87666-656-X
H-962

The elements of dog training are easy to grasp and apply, and this guide is for dog owners age 14 and older who are anxious to discover the secrets behind Lew Burke's methods.
Hard cover, 5½" x 8½", 255 pages 64 black and white photos, 23 full-color photos

DOG OWNER'S VETERINARY GUIDE
By G. W. Stamm
ISBN 0-87666-402-8
AP-927

The most accurate and up-to-date book based on recent information set forth by various notable veterinarians.
Hard cover, 5½" x 8", 112 pages 28 black and white photos, 39 line drawings

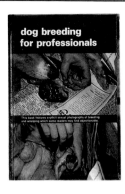

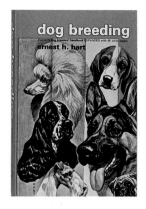

DOG BREEDING FOR PROFESSIONALS
By Dr. Herbert Richards
ISBN 0-87666-659-4
H-969

For dog owners who need and actively seek advice about how to go about breeding their dogs either for profit or purely because of their attachment to their animals. *Please note:* This book contains highly explicit photos of canine sexual activities that some readers may find offensive.
Hard cover, 5½ x 8½", 224 pages 105 black and white photos, 62 full-color photos, 4 charts

DOG BREEDING
By Ernest H. Hart
ISBN 0-87666-654-3
H-958

Easily understood and written for the breeder who is attempting to upgrade the quality of his representatives of a breed, this book covers every important aspect of breeding dogs, including both theory and completely practical day-to-day concerns. The physiology of the bitch and stud dog, gestation, whelping, fertility problems, how to build a strain,

breeding techniques, the selection of breeding partners, the importance of pedigrees, and environment and heredity are just some of the topics given ample treatment.
Hard cover, 5½ x 8½", 224 pages 77 black and white photos, 52 full-color photos

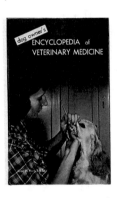

DOG OWNER'S ENCYCLOPEDIA OF VETERINARY MEDICINE
By Allan H. Hart, B.V.Sc.
ISBN 0-87666-287-4
H-934

Written by a veterinarian who feels that most dog owners should recognize the symptoms and understand the cures of most diseases of dogs so that they can properly communicate with their veterinarian.
Hard cover, 5½" x 8', 186 pages 86 black and white photos

DOGS FOR PROTECTION
By Lucine H. Flynn
ISBN 0-87666-813-9
PS-802

This book contains detailed information about choosing a dog to provide protection and about training dogs in the basic obedience routines that every protection dog must know. The author, a recognized expert in obedience teaching and judging, outlines step-by-step exercises for training a dog to be protective and alert, but not a snarling beast. This is a very practical volume.
Hard cover, 5½ x 8″, 96 pages
41 full-color photos, 29 black and white photos

THE COMPLETE DOG BUYERS' GUIDE
By Dr. William R. Bruette and Kerry V. Donnelly
ISBN 0-86622-026-7
H-1061

In one compact volume breeders, pet owners and other dog fanciers will find complete descriptions and information about many of the world's most popular dogs—over 120 breeds are listed! Each breed is fully described as to its history and development and is illustrated. The text includes a special pricing guide for the potential dog buyer. A great book for all dog lovers—invaluable for anyone looking for good advice about which breed to obtain.
Hard cover, 5½ x 8″; 608 pages
Contains 147 black and white photos

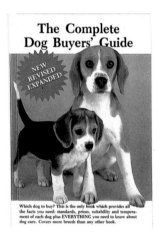

ILLUSTRATED TEXTBOOK OF DOG DISEASES
By The TV Vet
ISBN 0-87666-733-7
PS-770

For all dog owners, whether your pet is purebred or a mixed breed, who want general advice about how to keep their dogs healthy.
Hard cover, 5½″ x8″, 284 pages
380 black and white photos, 24 color photos